Writable

Self-Publishing Simplified

Nick Vulich

Author's Note

(Author's Note:

I originally published this book as **Indie Author's Toolbox**. In the three years since I released it self-publishing has done a complete 360. For the first time since their inception, eBook sales are down. Paper is back. And, so is audio. Draft2Digital has challenged Smashwords as the aggregator of choice. And, Barnes and Noble—does anyone buy books there?

Indie Author's Toolbox is back and newly revised and updated as **Writable: Self-Publishing Simplified**. Some readers are bound to ask, "why reprise a past work?" Or, "If it's already been published—Is there any reason for another go-around?"

That is a good question, and my answer simply is—Good Information Rises to the Top. It will help new authors sell more books and make more money with less time spent spinning their wheels. Experienced self-publishers can benefit, too, by gaining a new perspective on their day to day tasks.

If I am wrong—Amazon gives you seven days to get your money back—No Questions Asked.)

Contact me at

- E-mail: hi@nickvulich.com
- Blog: indieauthorstoolbox.com
- Blog: nickvulich.com

Table of Contents

One-Ply, or Two

I heard the greatest commercial ever a few years back.

NAPA Auto Parts compared choosing the right motor oil for your car to making a choice between one and two-ply tissue. I mean who thinks of this shit. No pun intended. It is brilliant. It is so in your face.

Everyone knows one ply can get the job done, but dammit—it can be messy at times as every tissue user knows. Two-ply offers that extra layer of security.

The connection makes it easy to make the leap from regular motor oil to synthetic oil. Yeah! It costs more, but the results are what count.

The promise is synthetic oil will help wipe away potential problems.

One-ply, or two-ply. It is a lifestyle choice.

I know. Some of you are thinking, what is the difference. I am just going to flush it down the drain. Might as well go cheap and save a few bucks. Right?

Let me stop you right now before you find yourself knee deep in a pile of doo-doo. Your choice of tissue speaks volumes about the kind of writer you are.

One ply users take things as they come.

These guys have no clue. They open a blank page in *Word* and fumble around while they wait for words to fill the screen. They fake it until they make it. They keep typing until their story comes together.

Two-ply authors are more calculating.

These guys have their shit together. Before they begin to write a new magazine article, blog post, or book—they plot everything out.

Before they have a single word committed to paper, they know how their story will end. These authors know who their main characters are, and their personality quirks. They know every plot twist and curve that will take place along the way.

Man! How I envy these guys.

I am sorry to say, I am not one of them.

Most of my books get their start in the **Notes** section of my *iPhone*. One minute I am driving along, and just like that, an idea pops into my head. It may be a sentence. A paragraph. A complete chapter.

It is not anything I can control.

When an idea hits, I get my ass off the road and start writing.

I approach book marketing the same way I do writing. Maybe I am reading a book or watching a movie. Then something goes off in my head.

- I should run a new Amazon Ad campaign.
- I should start a free book promotion.
- Book sales are down. I should book a *Kindle Count Down Deal* and advertise it on *BargainBooksy*, *Robin Reads*, etc.

You may be different. I do not know. The writing life is often solitary. You do not have coworkers or a back-office team to keep you on track.

Writing is a one-man business. You wear a lot of different hats. You are an author, publisher, copyeditor, proofreader, researcher, and clean-up specialist. As writers, we need to ensure that we provide our readers with the best possible experience. We need to wipe away our mistakes before they distract readers from our message.

This book is going to focus on book marketing. It talks about how to optimize your space on Amazon so that you can sell more books with less time and expense. Most of this is stuff you already know. If you are an old hand at writing and self-publishing, you are probably doing most of it already. If you are new to self-publishing, I am going to give you a lot of ideas. To get the best results, do not rush to try them all at once. Choose one or two ideas and run with them. When you are ready, dive into another project.

Some of the ideas will work for you, some of them will not. Some will work for one book, and not for another. I wish I could tell you beforehand which tips will be successful for you, and which ones will not. There is no way to tell in advance.

Go with it.

Getting Started

Are you having trouble picking the topic for your book? Maybe you finished writing your book, but you have questions about the mechanics of how to list it on Amazon. How do you write a compelling description? How do you know you chose the right cover? What are keywords anyway and why do they matter?

Did you publish a new book to the Kindle store and find yourself wondering what comes next?

You are not alone.

Publishing your first book or even your tenth book on Kindle is a daunting task. As an Indie author, you are going it alone or with limited help. That means you are responsible for everything about your book. You need to choose a topic that is going to sell. You need to write a compelling story that keeps readers flipping the pages. You need to ensure it is typo-free and formatted for a variety of Kindle devices and other e-readers. After that, you need to create a book cover, write your description, and choose keywords. And, let's not forget reviews.

Being an Indie Author can be scary at times. That is what this book is all about. It will help you move through the maze of publishing your book and getting it discovered on Kindle.

Choosing A Topic To Write About

Selecting a topic to write about is part art and part science.

Story ideas are all around you. Finding one that will sell is another story altogether. If you write nonfiction three topics are always in demand – health, wealth, and love. Fiction gets broken down into fads – chick lit, vampires, and zombies.

What I like about Amazon is they make it easy to become a bestseller in your category.

Here is why.

Amazon has over 4000 categories. When you dig deep down into each category, they number the top 100 bestsellers in each of them.

If you want to write a bestseller, this gives you over 400,000 opportunities.

Think about that for a moment. Most authors are never going to write a number one bestseller. It is unlikely they will ever make the top 100 bestseller list on Amazon. There is too much competition for those spots. For many authors, the subject matter of their book further limits these opportunities.

If you understand how Amazon works, it is easier to become a bestseller in your category. Maybe even a number one bestseller.

The good news for authors is you do not need to write a number one bestseller to pay the bills.

This section is going to help you choose a bestselling topic for your book.

Here are six techniques to help you research topics using Amazon.

1. Check out the books on Amazon's bestseller lists.
2. Read book descriptions for books like yours.
3. Use the "Look Inside" feature to read the first few chapters of books like yours.
4. Read book reviews to discover what people like and do not like about given books.
5. Look over the table of contents so that you better understand what your competitor's books are about.
6. Read the highlights. At the bottom of the book description page, Kindle shows the top highlights for each book. These are the sections people plan

on referring to again and again. If you do not do anything else, read the book highlights. They will help you discover what readers think is important.

Let's look at each of these topics in more detail.

Check out competing books on Amazon's bestseller lists.

This one should be a no-brainer. If you want to write a bestselling book, you need to understand what is currently selling.

Examine the top 100 books on the Kindle marketplace. Only look at paid books. You want to make money. These are the books readers are shelling out real cash for. Amazon also lets you search in the free store. Keep in mind; there is a difference between what people pay for and what they gobble up for free.

Fiction outsells nonfiction.

Fiction and nonfiction directed towards women sells better than books written for men. A recent study by *ComScore* noted that 56.6% of *Kindle* owners are female. Another survey by *Bowker* found that women buy three times as many books as men. If your books appeal to women, you have a better chance to sell more books.

When you examine titles on the bestseller lists, zero in on categories that interest you. Pay close attention to the top forty books in each category. Most readers will not look past the first page or two of results when they search for a book to read.

What you want to see as you look at categories is some books ranked under 30,000. The top one or two books in the category should rank under 20,000. No book in the top ten should rank over 50,000 in its category.

What these numbers tell you is there is a slight chance you might make some money. A book ranked under 10,000, sells around 20 books per day. A book ranked at 20,000, sells 7 to 10 copies per day, and a book ranked at 50,000, sells 2 or 3 books a day. If you price your book at $2.99, you have a shot at making between $200 to $1200 per month based on sales.

If most bestsellers in a category rank 100,000 or higher you should rethink your book idea. Even if you have something special to say, it is going to be a tough sell.

Read descriptions for books like yours. After you narrow your focus down, it is time to start looking at book descriptions.

What does the author say about the book? What benefits will the reader get from reading it? Does the description talk about the contents? Does it focus on learning a new skill? Keeping you entertained? Is the approach humorous? Educational? Or serious?

You need to get a feel for the book and how the author approaches the topic. It will help you narrow your focus, so you can distinguish your book from other books on the market.

Check out the description for this book. <u>Farthest North: America's First Arctic Hero and His Horrible, Wonderful Voyage of the Frozen Top of the World</u>. The description builds suspense. It outlines the position the members of the Advance were in. It tells how the entire world assumed the crew was dead in the Arctic cold. And, how Captain Elisha Kent Kane remained undaunted by the tragedies he faced.

The story is set up in four short paragraphs. There is a quick author bio and a list of his previous books followed by two glowing reviews.

It is an excellent description. It makes you want to read more. For an author who intends to write about a similar topic you quickly learn what you are up against.

Use the "Look Inside" feature to see what competitor books are about.

Pay attention to the Introduction or "Why You Need to Read This Book" section. The introduction tells you what topics the author feels are unique about his book. Often, authors of nonfiction books lay out the steps or methods they are going to follow to solve a problem.

As you read through the first few chapters, study the content. Make notes about the subjects it covers. Pay close attention to the author's tone. Is it conversational, like he is talking to a friend? Is it boastful, helpful, or more authoritative?

The author's tone is just as important as what he says. If the book is boastful, reviews reflect this. Many say, "all the author could talk about was himself." If the author writes in an authoritative tone, the reviews may say his style is "condescending." "He talks way over your head."

Pay attention to the writing style and tone of competing books. Use that information to craft the proper voice for your book.

Read reviews for books like yours. What do people like about the book? What don't they like? Reviewers are not afraid to say what they think. Use these reviews to develop a better and more complete book. When you write your book description, tell readers about your book. Let them know it contains the information they have been asking for.

Study competitor reviews. They tell you exactly what to write.

One of the books I am thinking about here is Zealot: The Life and Times of Jesus of Nazareth by Reza Asian. The book has 3,000 reviews. Over ten percent of them are one-star. The reviews tell you why the book is wrong. They say where its thesis went wrong. They say what the author should have talked about or used as evidence.

You could write a dozen or more books based on the adverse comments for this book. The reviews give you all the information you need to write a follow-up bestseller.

Read the table of contents. The table of contents is a goldmine of information for authors. A quick glance through it shows you what content the book covers. They suggest how to organize your topic. They make it easy to see what topics other authors decided weren't important enough to include.

When I page through the table of contents, I get ideas for new books. One book had a short chapter on selling books. It barely scratched the surface of what is involved. After giving it some thought, it turned into my book – How to Make Money Selling Old Books and Magazines on eBay. I read a book about social media that briefly mentioned the new *Twitter Vine App*. Those three paragraphs morphed into my book – *Twitter Vine App Explained*.

The table of contents reveals what information the author chose not to include. Use these points as ammunition to add value to your book. If you take exception to the conclusions, explain why you disagree. Explain why your idea is better. Doing this distinguishes your book from others.

If you are unsure how to do this, read: They Say / I Say: The Moves That Matter in Persuasive Writing by Gerald Graff and Cindy Birkenstein. It is geared towards grad students and explains how to frame arguments for academic papers. Consider it a whack on the side of the head to get your creative juices flowing. The ideas contained in this one book may spawn a bunch of book ideas for you.

Michael Alvear used this contrarian strategy to create a killer book title. Make a Killing on Kindle (Without Blogging, Facebook, or Twitter). Every book about self-publishing up to that point said social media was critical. They suggested you had to blog, comment on Facebook and Twitter, and connect with readers. The implication was if you did not do those things your book would not sell. Alvear's book boldly challenged that theory.

Read the book highlights. Kindle displays the top highlights at the bottom of each book description page. Readers highlight text that is important to them or they want to refer to later. Kindle makes highlights more relevant by listing how many readers highlighted each comment.

To do quick research on a Kindle book scan through the contents. Read the highlights first. This tells you what readers thought was important. If 200 users highlight a section on eBay listing descriptions, people want to know about it. If 150 users highlight a section about how to use the *Send to Kindle App*, readers want to know more about it.

Make a note of the important highlights. Include content about them in your book. Turn some of the highlighted content into a stand-alone book or guide. If 200 readers took the time to highlight something, there is a keen interest in the topic. If you need further validation, check blogs and forums. If people are talking about the issue there, you have a winner.

Author Central Explained

Amazon created Author Central to showcase information about authors and their books.

One thing we know: If people like your book they are going to want to know more about you. What you look like; how you got started writing; where you live; and what other books you have published.

To claim your Author Central page, visit the following link:

https://authorcentral.amazon.com/gp/home?ie=UTF8&pn=iri d37437482

Upload an author biography to introduce yourself. Add a picture so readers can have a look at your bright and smiling face. Author Central gives you a place to collect all your books in one place so readers can browse through them.

Each time you publish a new book click on Add Book, to add your latest title to your list of books.

You can link your blog and Twitter account to your Author Central Account. When you do this, your recent tweets show up with highlights from your three most recent blog posts.

You can upload book trailers or promotional videos. If you are good with video, create a series of videos so readers can learn more about you and your books.

Many writers link their books to their Facebook fan page or their author website. A link to Author Central might pay off better over the long haul. Not only does it introduce readers to you, but it also gives you an opportunity to sell more books.

The next section explores Author Central in more detail. Use it to set up a profile that sells you and your books.

Claim your books

Author Central gives you a spot to collect all your books in one location where fans can easily find them.

To claim your books, click on the Books tab in the Author Central banner. Doing this displays a page that shows Books by your name. Below this, you will see a yellow button that says Add more books. Click on it and paste in the ISBN of your book. You can also type your name or the title of your book and search for it that way.

When Amazon shows your book, confirm that it is your title to add it to your list of books.

When you publish a new book add it so that readers can quickly locate your book.

Author Bio

Your author bio gives you another chance to sell yourself and your books.

Match your bio to your writing style. If you write humorous books, comedies or satire make your bio light and breezy. If you write authority books, use your bio to position yourself as an expert in your field. Talk about your advanced degrees, years of experience, awards, and other publications.

A lot of novelist talk about themselves, their family, their pets or what inspires them to write.

The key is to make your author bio unique and informative. Think of it as your elevator pitch. Answer these questions – Who are you? What do you do? How can readers benefit from reading your books?

How to write a great author bio

As writers, we regularly promote ourselves and do what we can to put our books in front of new readers.

The problem is a lot of authors take the shotgun approach. They blast their message out to everyone in the hopes that a few people will act on it. It is possible one or two readers may look. Some users may drop $2.99 to buy your book, but the odds are it is going to miss its mark with most of the people you want to reach.

You are casting too wide of a net. When you target everyone, you are likely to miss the folks who would be most interested your book. Sean Platt and Johnny B. Truant put it best in <u>Write. Publish. Repeat.</u> They say to tell your story. Go into detail about your ideal reader. Tell readers who your book is for and who it is not for and do not worry about turning away a bunch of potential readers. You are better off finding your true followers. Over the long haul, it is going to save you a lot of grief and negative reviews. Readers who are not a good match for your message or your writing style tend to leave more one-star reviews.

You need to develop a brand statement. Sum up what you are all about in one sentence.

I write short easy to put in place solutions that help readers solve e-commerce problems. As a result, they can sell more stuff on eBay, Amazon, Etsy and Fiverr. That is a good start at my brand statement. Over time I have narrowed it down even further. My goal is to make it as easy as possible for readers to understand what I am all about.

Here is what I finally came up with –

Short easy to read solutions to your e-commerce problems.

That is my entire brand statement. Nine easy words tell readers all they need to know to decide if I am the guy they are looking for.

How about you?

Can you sum up your brand in less than ten words? If not, take a good look at what you are doing because if you cannot easily define yourself—neither can your readers.

When you define your brand this way, it keeps you focused on what is important to your readers. Each of my books needs to be short, easy to understand and solve one e-commerce problem. If each book does that I fulfill the promise I made to my readers.

My brand statement is the opening line to my author biography. After it, I add a sentence or two to flesh it out, so readers can get a better idea of what my books are about.

Here is the long version.

Short easy to read solutions to your e-commerce problems.

Most of my books can be read in under an hour. The information in them can help you sell more products on eBay and Amazon. It can help you sell services on Fiverr or eBooks and books on Amazon and Kindle.

Let me ask you again. What is your short and long brand statement?

Write it out. Incorporate it into your author bio. It will sell a lot of books for you.

Writable: Self-Publishing Simplified

Profile picture

I would rather go to the dentist and have a tooth pulled than have my picture taken. But, readers want to see your picture. They want to know what you look like. They want to know that you are a real person.

When you post your picture on Author Central, it can help you sell more books.

It is crazy but true.

Look at other author pictures in your genre. If they are all suited up, you should be too. If they dress in business casual, go with that. A lot of authors like to pose with their kids or their pets. That is ok too, especially if you write fiction. If you write about business or more serious topics, go for the suit.

Sports writers can get away with wearing a team jersey. Diet and exercise gurus would look best in shorts or sweats.

Pay someone to take the background out of the picture. Just include your figure. It looks more professional.

Tailor your author picture to what you write. But, make sure it reflects your personality. If your shiny red Beamer is the light of your life—snap a picture of you sitting behind the wheel. Or, it could be a picture of you kneeling beside the open driver's side door.

Your picture tells readers who you are and what is special about you.

Add your Twitter feed & recent blog posts

You can build your brand by linking your Twitter feed and recent blog posts to your Amazon Author page. When you do this, your Author page displays recent Tweets and your most recent blog posts.

To add your blog or Twitter feed, go to Author Central. Select add multimedia, blog feeds, a Twitter feed. Click where it says Author Central Profile. Towards the bottom of the page, there is a section labeled blogs. Click at the top where it says to add a blog.

Paste the RSS feed from your blog here, not your blog URL. If you host your blog on Blogger, scroll down to the bottom of your blog where it says Subscribe to Posts. When you click on this, it displays a bunch of code in your browser window. Ignore that. Scroll up to the address bar. Highlight the URL, copy and paste it into the box.

If you use WordPress to host your blog, the location of your RSS feed is going to depend upon the template you use. After you locate the correct link, do the same thing. Click on the Subscribe to Post option or RSS Feed. Paste the URL from the browser address bar into the box on your Amazon Author page.

Adding your Twitter feed is much easier. After you add your blog, you see a column labeled Twitter. It is over to the far-right side of the page. Click where it says Edit account. It brings up a box that asks you to type in your Twitter username. As soon you do this your most recent Tweet appears to the right of your author bio. Be patient. It can take a few days for blog posts and tweets to begin displaying.

If you are a "Doubting Thomas" and think what is the point? Why should I waste my time with all that BS?

My best answer is readers want to know more about you. They want to know who you are, what you are doing, and what comes next.

If you provide the information, they will come.

Need more proof?

I ran a Kindle Countdown Deal last week. When I checked my blog stats, it had over one thousand-page views. Most days I average fifty to seventy-five.

That is a lot more eyes on my stuff. It is nine hundred extra shots to get readers to join my email list.

I will take that any day.

Add events

The events section lets you add speaker engagements, book signings, and conferences.

When you fill out this section it makes it easier for fans to connect with you in person. It reinforces your authority platform by positioning you as an expert. When readers learn you are a featured speaker at conferences, they assume you know your stuff.

Add photos and videos

These two sections let you add a visual element to your profile. I added my picture and some book covers. Some authors upload pictures of themselves, their pets or their family. Other authors display photos that complement their books. Look at what other authors in your category are doing. Upload the pictures that you feel best represent your brand.

People love videos. There is no question about that.

I had Professor Hans Von Puppet of Fiverr fame make a video to promote one of my books. I also had a whiteboard video done to promote several of my books. I uploaded them to YouTube and linked them to Author Central.

Some authors record a welcome video. Other authors make elaborate video trailers. Like photos, videos are a personal preference. Experiment with different videos to see what works best for you.

If you are comfortable working with video, make a series of short how-to videos. They do not need to be more than two to five minutes long and would make a great lead into your books.

You could have someone conduct a short interview with you about one of your books. Talk about why you write, or a charity you support. Choose something that draws readers into your story. It does not have to be about you or your books. Just ensure it reflects your message.

Author Central can even help you spy on your competition. They have a section that shows readers other authors who write similar books.

Bookmark these authors. Read their books. Study their book descriptions and author bio. Hell! You may even want to buy a few of their books from time to time. It could open an entirely new world of possibilities for you. You could discover a hole in their catalog that lets you jump in and add a new title.

Recently, some authors have teamed up to promote their books. They drop their book prices to 99¢ for a day or a weekend. They take a group shot of the book covers, then each author posts about the special on their blog or website. To supercharge things, even more, they mention the promotion on Facebook and Twitter. Authors who have done this have built some real momentum for their books.

What about you?

It is easy to get started. Email other authors in your genre or a similar category. Tell them you want to run a promotion with them and several other writers. Explain how it could benefit everyone by allowing you to reach a larger audience.

Are you still unconvinced or need some more ideas to make it work?

- Horror writers could promote a spooktacular around Halloween or Friday the 13th.
- Romance writers could offer a Valentine's love fest

- History writers could promote books around holidays or current events.

No matter what genre you write in there is a holiday or something special going on that you can promote around. Strap on your thinking cap. Dream up new ideas. Sell more books.

Reports, Reviews, and More

Author Central keeps you up-to-date on your author rank and recent reviews.

The blue tab at the top of the page displays six headings. Home, Books, Profile, Sales Info, Rank, Customer Reviews, and Help.

Home is a quick overview. It shows links to other Amazon sites – Audible, CreateSpace and Kindle Direct Publishing. It contains links to update your profile and book lists.

Books lets you add books to your bibliography. Select add books and follow the prompts.

This section lets you add more content to your Amazon book description page.

To get started, click on the book you want to update. In the upper right corner of the page, there is a list of the different formats the book is available in. Paperback, Hardback, Kindle, Audible, and any other editions. You need to add content to each of them. If your book is available in three formats, you need to go into each of them and post the information.

When you click on the Books tab, it shows three tabs – Editorial Reviews, Book Details, and Book Extras.

Editorial Reviews lets you add more content to your book's description page. A few of these sections do not apply to eBooks. I am going cover their intended use. Then I will give you a few ideas about how you can make the most of them so that you can sell more books.

Reviews. The best use of this section is to highlight your top three of four reviews. Do not post the whole review. Pick out one or two key sentences. Emphasize key points in italic. List the author's name in bold below it.

Product description. You can post your book description here or in KDP when you upload your book.

From the author. Talk about yourself. Talk about your book or take a few moments to introduce the subject matter of your book. I posted a self-interview in this section for all my eBay books. It gave me the opportunity to tell readers why they should sell on eBay and how to get started. **FYI**: This is prime real estate. Information posted here displays on your book description page. It shows up below the customers who bought this item also bought section.

Make every word you put here count.

From the inside flap. This section is a leftover from traditionally published books. The information on the inside flap goes here. eBooks do not have an inside flap, so it gives you an opportunity to get a little creative. I use it to talk about the changing nature of eBay and how my books can help you to sell more in this volatile climate.

From the back cover. This section displays the information from the back flap. As an eBook author, use it to your advantage. Too many eBay books promise readers they can become a millionaire overnight. They tell readers you can get rich working five hours a week. I let them know it does not work that way. You can make a decent living selling on eBay, but it takes hard work. Doing this distinguishes me from the get rich quick scammers and con artists out there.

About the author. Your author bio from Author Central displays on your book description page. For some books, you may want to use a different version of your bio. That is where this section can come in handy. I write about many different e-commerce topics. When I write about job search, I include a different bio that focuses on how I help clients in their career search. When I write about social media, my author bio reflects my expertise in that area.

Many experts suggest you should not bother filling in the above sections. They say it is information overload. It confuses readers. These are the same guys who say you should keep your book description short. Their thought is your book description should not be longer than two or three paragraphs. My thought is that is a waste of prime real estate. You need to tell more to sell more.

It is true. Most readers scan through your book description to find information that interests them. There are also a lot of readers who hang on every word. They check every detail before they make a purchase – even if it is a 99¢ eBook.

The key takeaway from all this is to be creative. Use the different sections to include information that will help sell your book. Include short excerpts. Profile your main characters. If your setting is in a foreign country or exotic locale, talk about the customs there.

Have fun with it.

Switch it up a little. Change the information you include on your book description page from time to time. Market researchers say people need to hear your message eight times before they buy. Give them something different to look at each time they come back to your book description page.

Book details are something you cannot change. It lists the publisher, date of publication, the number of pages, and such.

Book extras apply more to fiction. You add the content here using Shelfari.

You can discuss your top three characters. Give a simple outline of your plot. Add quotations from your book. If you write science fiction or fantasy, add a glossary to help readers understand your book. There is also a section where you can add any awards your book has won.

You do not have to add any of this content. It is extra information that can help sell your book. If you are uncomfortable getting started, you can baby-step it. Add one section today and another in a few weeks or months when you are ready.

The Sales Info tab lets authors keep track of their paperback and hardbound sales. Book Scan reports the sales and updates them every Friday. They explain not all sales get included in these numbers. The info tab says only 75% of your book sales get reported. That sounds about right to me. I publish all my books through CreateSpace. The numbers do not match up with Book Scan. Amazon does not report expanded-distributions sales right away. They wait until the distributor pays for them.

Rank displays your author standing on Amazon. You can get a snapshot of your sales rank for all books or Kindle only.

You can also dig down into categories for the ranking in each category you write in. Use this tool to track your growth in a category. Each time you add a new book, it should nudge your ranking up a notch or two.

Customer reviews show up here two or three days after they post on Amazon. It is an easier way to read them than checking your book page. This section gives you the option to comment on book reviews. But, I would not recommend doing that. Some authors like to say thank you for five-star reviews. Some authors get caught up commenting on bad reviews. Nothing good can come from this. The best strategy is to read your reviews. Take what you can from them and move on.

   The Help tab explains in more detail how to use Author Central. If you have any questions, it answers most of them for you.

Amazon Book Optimization

Psst! Do you want to know a secret?

There are no secrets. No tricks. No magical incantations you can invoke to sell more books on Amazon or any other online book site.

Selling more books is all about how you manage the basics.

You need to –

1. Write a good book
2. Select a killer title
3. Create an attention-grabbing cover
4. Write a book description that compels readers to click the buy button
5. Choose keywords that drive searchers to your book
6. Ensure your "look inside" sample sells your book

If you execute these six steps well your book is going to sell. Misfire on any of them, and you're going to have problems.

Some of the advice I give you here goes contrary to what the "experts" say. During my five years as an Indie author/self-publisher, I have taken a lot of wrong turns. I got a lot of bad advice starting out. All I can tell you is what has worked best for me. The best advice I can give you is to experiment often. Do not be afraid to try new things. Keep the ones that work. Discard the ones that do not. Keep building your bag of tricks. Over time you will develop a system that works for you.

With that said, let's dig deeper into each step to see how you can use them to position your book for success.

Write a good book. Abraham Lincoln said it best. "You can fool all the people some of the time, and some of the people all the time, but you cannot fool all the people all the time."

If your book sucks, the reviews are going to catch up with you. Then people will stop buying your book. Sure. You can sell a few copies of a bad book. Sometimes you can sell a whole lot of copies. Eventually, the reviews are going to kill your career.

There are a lot of Kindle advice writers that tell aspiring authors you do not have to write well. That you should not waste too much time editing your work. Just do the best you can. Get your book out there. Sell a few copies. Then write your next book.

Last year, or the year before, that advice might have worked. But, readers are getting smarter. They have downloaded a lot of worthless crap over the past few years. They are tired of it. If you do not believe me, read the reviews. Most readers are honest. They call it as they see it. If your book smells like a load of horse hockey, readers are going to say it. If enough readers jump on the bandwagon, there is no going back.

Forget the writing advice books that tell you how quickly you can write a book. You cannot write a book before breakfast. You cannot write it over your lunch break, or on a roll of toilet paper while you are sitting on the throne. Forget the books that tell you-you can write a book in seven days, twenty-one days or even thirty days. The fact is you can write a book in the time it takes you—no sooner and no later.

There is a disconnect between what readers want and what writers think they want. Many writers believe readers want to read short books. Reviewers say the opposite. Here are a few of the reviews major novelists recently received for their Kindle Shorts.

- A throw away sixty pages. Lee Child
- Don't waste time and money buying the ads, wait for the book itself. Janet Evanovich
- It's so short; it isn't even a short story. Dean Koontz.

- Good writing for the beginning of a novel, with no real ending. Steven King

No matter what anyone tells you most readers do not like short. It makes them feel like they missed out on something or that the writer was out to take their money. Consider this the next time you go to publish a short manuscript.

The key to selling more books is to write a complete book that leaves readers satisfied. If you do this, you are golden. Readers will leave enthusiastic reviews. They will tell their friends about you. They will race out to buy your books the day they get released.

Select a killer title. Too many writers try to stuff a load of keywords into their title in the hopes that they can game the system. Search engines may find keyword bloated titles enticing. Real readers get turned off by titles too big to fit on the book cover.

They cannot remember them. They do not understand them. They do not know what to think about books that use them.

Short is best.

One to three words is the perfect length for a title. It is easy to remember. There is less chance for confusion. As a result, you are going to sell more books.

Check out the following five titles. They are short. They are memorable. They reveal what the book is about. And, if I did not mention it they are selling a lot of books.

- *Story $elling* by Nick Nanton & J. W. Dicks
- *eBay Seller Secrets* by Ann Eckhart
- *Declutter your Inbox* by S. J. Scott
- *Killing Jesus* by Bill O'Reilly
- *Email Marketing Blueprint* by Steve Scott

Compare that to these titles.

- *7 Steps to Sales Scripts for B2B Appointment Setting* by Scott Channell
- *How I Make Money Every Day Automatically When Others Sell on eBay* by Xavier Zimms
- *Author's Quick Guide to Making Money with your 99¢ Kindle Books* by Kristen Eckstein
- *How to Write and Publish your Book on Amazon and on Kindle* by Eldes Saullo
- *How to Write a Kindle Book that People Want to Buy before Breakfast* by James Bedford

Use your primary keyword in your title. If you can, begin your title with your most relevant keyword. You will rank higher in search. Use a combination of two or three keywords. Do not string together a series of two or three keyword phrases in your title. It does not make sense.

Instead, write a short title. Follow it up with an excellent subtitle. It should tell readers a little more about the subject matter of your book. Once again, keep the subtitle short. Less than ten words are best. Include your most relevant keywords in your title and subtitle. Place your other search terms where they belong – in your book tags and your description.

Make your cover sizzle. Three things attract readers to your book – the title, the cover, and the synopsis.

Whatever you do, do not design your cover yourself. No matter how good you think you are, or how great you think your idea is, do not create your cover. Do not let your best friend or baby sister do it either. Your cover is too important to leave to chance.

I am a serial Fiverr. I outsourced 179 graphic design gigs on Fiverr over the past six months. Some of the work you receive is so-so. But a lot of Fiverr gigs deliver professional quality designs. The results, like anything else, depend on the effort you put into it.

You can also outsource your cover on Elance, 99 Designs, or Upwork. They have experienced graphic designers who can help you create a professional cover.

The key to getting a great deign is to know what you want before you select a designer. Look at other books in your genre. Do not steal anyone else's design. Instead, look for a common theme that runs through the book covers in your genre. If you find something you like, download that cover and send it to your designer. Tell them you like this cover but have a few ideas to change it up and make it your own. You can also send your designer three or four covers you like to let them know this is the style you want.

Sometimes I know what I want. If that is the case, I put together a short sketch. Other times, I tell the designer to run with it. If I do not have any idea what I want, I pick four or five designers to create the initial concept. If I do not like the designs that come back, I try again. Sometimes I like different portions of several covers. Then I have one of the designers put it all together for me.

Most recently, I have been more concerned with controlling the images used on my book covers. Many designers on Fiverr hit you with an upcharge to buy clipart, but you never know. If they grab a piece of art without the proper license, it is your butt that is on the line for a lawsuit. Another issue I have run into is I do not remember which designer I used to make some of my earlier covers. This creates problems when I release audiobook and paperback versions of my book. I do not know where to buy clipart rights for the newer versions of those covers.

Because of this, I source most of the clipart before I give the project to a designer. This way I know, I am legal and hold the proper licenses for all the artwork used on my covers. I get most of my clipart from Can Stock Photo. http://www.canstockphoto.com/ Or, Shutterstock. https://www.shutterstock.com. The prices are reasonable and range from $2.50 to $10.00 per use.

After I choose images, I put together specific instructions for the cover designer.

I would like a book cover for an Audible audiobook. The cover size is 2500 x 2500 pixels. It needs to be a perfect square, and all the text and images need to fit it. You cannot stretch out the original book cover to fit the space. They will reject the cover.

I am enclosing the original clipart and a copy of the original book cover. Please keep as close to the original design as possible.

Specify the exact cover size. Designers seem to deliver eBook covers in slightly different dimensions. When you order a CreateSpace cover, tell the designer you want a .pdf file. Make sure they conform to CreateSpace sizing guidelines. Several designers have delivered the paperback cover as a jpeg. Of course, it was unusable.

When you order a CreateSpace cover, your designer needs extra information. You need to specify the trim size (example: 6 x 9). They also need to know the paper style, and how many pages are in your book. Your designer requires all this information to size your cover. You also need to supply any text or illustrations for the back-cover blurb. If you want to print on the spine, you need to specify the text. **FYI**: Your book needs to be at least 120 pages to have room for written message on the spine.

If you are unsure about your cover or your book concept have several covers ready to go. That way if your book gets off to a slow start you can switch covers to see if the new one sells more copies.

Write a compelling book description.

Congratulations. You did it. You wrote an impressive title. You created a dazzling book cover. Now it is time to close the deal.

How do you turn browsers into buyers?

A compelling book description can get readers drooling for more.

There is no right or wrong way to write a book description.

Some authors start off by asking a question. Others present a dilemma their main character finds themselves in. Still, others summarize their story. Any of these approaches can work.

You need to draw readers into your story. Get them hooked on your story or in the case of nonfiction, on the solution you are presenting. Make it interesting. Create suspense. Make them want to read more.

How do you do that?

Ask questions.

Have you ever wondered what life would be like if you took the other road? The one your parents, teachers, and friends told you would put you on a collision course with the others? What if you veered a little off course for just a few minutes? Would it change your destiny forever?

Make your case as an authority figure.

Nick has a unique combination of experience and knowledge. This helps him guide new and experienced sellers through the maze we call eBay.

Introduce your main character.

Max Power stood at the crossroads of now and forever. If he followed her into the time portal, everything would disappear forever. If he took the leap, his future was uncertain. All Max knew for certain was the girl had saved his life back on Zeta 9. Now she was offering him a future as uncertain as the Zondervan Divide.

Compare your writing to a famous author.

Reviewers say my writing is a cross between Stephen King and Peter Straub with a touch of Kurt Vonnegut thrown in for comedy relief. Read *Death Race 3000*. Find out for yourself why the Zombie Jesus challenged the Werewolf Devil. Laugh your ass off. Puke your guts out. Run the full gamut of your emotions. You may never want to read another book again – Ever!

F A B Approach.

Use the use the F – A – B approach to make more sales. Tell them the Features, Advantages, and Benefits of reading your book.

For example:

- **Feature**: This book offers a simple step-by-step plan to succeed in selling on eBay.
- **Advantage**: What this means to you is you will have a detailed and tested plan to follow.

- **Benefit**: So that you can easily make $100 a day or more selling on eBay.

The beauty of the F – A – B System is it makes everything easy for the reader to understand. In this example, you are offering, "a simple step-by-step plan to succeed on eBay." Follow up and tell the reader, "What this means to you." (You need to tell them, do not ever assume they get it). "Is you will have a detailed and tested plan to follow." Sounds good so far, but you still need to tell them what is in it for them. You need to tell them what following your system will do for them. In this case, it means they "can easily make $100 a day or more selling on eBay."

Let's look at another example:

- **Feature**: The weight loss advice in this book allows you to eat all the foods you like.
- **Advantage**: You will not feel deprived of your favorite foods and get the urge to cheat on your diet.
- **Benefit**: As a result, you will be more likely to follow through with the plan and drop those pounds you want to lose.

In the weight loss example, you tell readers they can eat all the foods they like. Most people (at this point) are going to think that is great but how can it be true. And, you offer the advantage because you will, "get the urge to cheat on your diet." Follow up with the benefit to let them know what is in it for them. "You are more likely to follow through with the plan." So, it will be easier for you to drop the pounds you want to lose.

You can add more information and explain some of the details of your plan. The best way to do this is with a series of bullet points. Lists make it easy for readers to find the information they need. Lists are easy to scan. Readers can go right to the points that interest them.

Another method is to use bold headlines to break out your offer.

- Under each headline include two or three short sentences that describe your offer.
- The key is to make it easy for readers to go right to the information that interests them.

When you write a nonfiction book description, remember, it is all about the reader. Show readers you can help them get what they want, and you will have them eating out of your hands.

Choose keywords that attract buyers. The easiest way to understand keywords is to think of them as mini billboards. They drive searchers to your books.

Amazon has several areas where you can add keywords to optimize traffic to your book.

1. The book title and subtitle
2. The book description

3. The search keywords you enter when you upload your book

If you are new to keyword optimization your first question is probably what are keywords? Where do you find keywords to describe your book?

A lot of the "experts" send you to the Google Keywords tool, but that is not necessary. What we are trying to do here is optimize your book for Amazon. The best way to do that is to discover what search terms Amazon readers use to find books like yours.

Nine times out of ten, I select most of my search terms using the Amazon search bar. It shows me the terms readers use to find similar books on Amazon.

If I am writing a Kindle book, I go to the Amazon search bar, click on the arrow at the left-hand side, and select Kindle Store. The first thing I type in is my general search term. In this case—eBay.

What pops up is –

- eBay in Kindle Store
- eBay in all departments
- eBay in Apps for Android
- eBay selling
- eBay for Dummies
- eBay .com
- eBay business
- eBay garage sale
- eBay home

- eBay books
- eBay store
- eBay 2014

These are the search terms readers use to find your book. *eBay for Dummies* and *eBay 2014* are off limits because they are titles of books in the category. It is against Amazon's TOS to use book titles or author names in your search keywords.

Examine the rest of the list. I would use eBay selling, eBay business, eBay garage sale, eBay books, and eBay store.

Next, type in "eBay" followed by each letter of the alphabet. Cull out search terms you think would be relevant to your book.

Here are some of the other keywords I came up with

- eBay Amazon
- eBay arbitrage
- eBay buying and selling
- eBay Basics
- eBay consignment
- eBay Clothing
- eBay drop shipping
- eBay guide
- eBay how to
- eBay income
- eBay power seller
- eBay shipping

This gives us seventeen solid keywords readers use to search for Kindle books. You can further confirm these keywords by examining book titles and descriptions.

Type "eBay" into the Amazon search bar. Select the first book. Go down to the product details section. Most books rank in two or three categories. Choose the category labeled eBay This takes you to the eBay bestsellers.

Look through the titles and descriptions of the books listed. What keywords appear in all the titles and subtitles. The authors decided these were the most relevant. Use this info to narrow down your search terms.

Ensure that your "look inside" sample closes the deal. It is the top of the ninth and the bases are loaded. The suspense is building. Can you convert lookers into buyers?

You are batting 100 so far.

Your cover, title, and keywords convinced readers to click on your book. They read your description, but something is holding them back. Should they buy it? Should they search for another book? Or, should they take a "look inside" to see what your book is all about?

The "Look Inside" section is your last chance to seal the deal and get readers to press the buy button. You need to ensure your "look inside" sample puts your best foot forward.

If you write fiction, make it suspenseful. Do not waste words laying out scenes or scenarios. Jump right into your story. Come out with both guns blazing. Keep the action building. End your sample on a cliffhanger where readers need to buy the book to discover what happens next.

If you write nonfiction, open your book with a "Why you need to read this book" section. Outline the problem you are going to solve. Present the steps you are going to take to relieve your reader's pain. Follow this up with a short "About me" section. Introduce yourself, and your qualifications. Say why you are the best guy to solve their problem.

This is where longer books have a real advantage.

Amazon samples the first ten percent of your book in the "look inside" feature. If your book is short, prospective readers only get to read one or two pages of your book. That is going to make it a tough sell. You want readers to see your table of contents and read at least eight to ten pages of your book. The more they read, the more likely it is they will buy your book.

A good sample is your best salesman.

On Amazon Promotions

Amazon gives you several ways to promote your book. Some, like KDP Free Days, Kindle Countdown Deals, and price are under your control. Others, like promotional boxes and direct mail newsletters, get determined by Amazon. They slot your book by how well it sells.

I am going to talk a little about each of these methods, and how you can best use them to sell more books on Amazon.

KDP Free Days are the first thing most authors think about when the talk turns to on Amazon promotions. There has been a lot of talk recently that KDP Free Days are not what they used to be and there is some truth to that. But, a lot of authors have been able to launch or revive their books using KDP Free Days.

Kindle Countdown Deals are another proven promotional tool. Amazon introduced them as a way for authors to promote their books without giving away the farm. You can discount your book for up to seven days in every ninety-day period. And, the best part is, even if you promote your book for 99 cents—you still get paid the full 70% royalty, not 35%.

Kindle Unlimited lets readers sample your books without any risk. Amazon members who enroll in Kindle Unlimited can read all the books they want for a small fee of only $9.99 per month. The problem for authors is Kindle Unlimited downloads have skyrocketed. They make up fifty to seventy percent of sales in many categories. At .0058 cents per page read that eats away at your author earnings.

Price is a promotional tool you have available to you every day. Many writers keep their book sales steady by cycling prices. When sales are good, they leave their book prices at $2.99 or $3.99. When sales slow-down, they drop their book prices to 99¢ for from three to seven days to get sales moving again.

These are all promotions you affect and can set into motion at any time.

Once your book begins to sell, Amazon's promotional algorithms kick in. The more books you sell, the harder Amazon works to promote your book.

When your book first gets released, it can hit one of the three Hot New Releases spots at the top of Amazon's sales page. In some categories, as few as one to two sales per day will win you the box. In more competitive categories it may take thirty or more sales per day. It also comes down to luck. If you release your book when fewer new titles are in the mix, it makes it easier for your book to rank.

Books are only eligible to be on the Hot New Releases list for thirty days after publication. Some authors game the system by changing the release date of their book every month. This way they can stay on the Hot New Releases list for two or three months rather than one. Should you do it? Probably not. If Amazon finds out, they can delete your book or close your Kindle account.

The more books you sell, the more Amazon promotes them. If enough copies sell, it gets displayed in the Customers who bought this item also bought section. This spot gives your book more exposure to readers who may have an interest in it. The more books you sell, the more Amazon will promote your book.

Amazon also sends out promotional emails several times per week. Sometimes they promote one book, and other times they push a group of similar books. When your book gets on one of these lists, it can mean a lot of extra sales.

Again, you can only affect Amazon's promotions indirectly. Amazon's marketing engine runs on sales. Some authors try to game the system. They join groups of authors that agree to buy each other's books to try and raise their sales rank. Other writers buy fifty or one hundred copies of their book all at once. They think this will increase their rank. The problem is Amazon has caught on to this game. Multiple purchases over a short period count as a single sale. This keeps authors from gaming the system.

Lesson learned: Only real sales count. Quit trying to game the system. Concentrate on marketing your books to real readers.

KDP Free Days

KDP Free Days can help launch your book and reinvigorate sluggish sales.

There is a lot of talk among authors that free has lost its allure. That books no longer enjoy the sales bump they used to enjoy after a great free run. Part of that is right, but it does not mean running a free promo cannot help your book.

It means you need to understand better what results you can expect to receive from your free run.

When you launch a new book, free is still the best way to get the word out. It can get people reading and talking about your book.

If you have already run through two or three KPD Free Promos, free may no longer be the best option. With so many new books hitting the Amazon catalog every day it is getting harder and harder to get noticed. With the changes to how free books count towards sales numbers, a free promo will not give your book the sales bump you want.

Most authors today agree you cannot select a free promo and expect downloads to follow. You need to promote your KDP Free Days.

That means you need to blog about your free promo days. You need to jump on Facebook and Twitter to help spread the word. Some authors buy ads on BookBub, Pixel of Ink and other favorite sites.

I have seen list after list of sites where you can promote your free books. The problem is these sites come and go, so lists go out of date almost as soon as they get posted. An easier way to promote your book is to buy four or five Fiverr gigs and let them do the promotional work for you. Doing this saves you time, frustration, and wasted emails.

Here are some of the better Fiverr gigs I have used.

http://www.fiverr.com/koky1205/submit-your-free-kindle-book-to-20-best-kindle-promotion-

http://www.fiverr.com/mlmauthor/promote-your-free-kindle-book

http://www.fiverr.com/thedesertgirl/submit-your-free-kindle-book-to-12-promo-sites

http://www.fiverr.com/bknights/submit-your-free-kindle-book-to-the-15-best-kindle-promotion-sites

http://www.fiverr.com/timmybx/manually-submit-your-kdp-kindle-ebook-free-day-promo-to-15-kindle-book-sites

So, what should an author do?

Remember, KDP is only one option in your toolbox.

Steve Scott published a short book called <u>Is 99 Cents the New Free?</u> For several months after its publication, authors sampled their catalog at 99 cents.

Jordan Malik made a hell of a run using 99 cent promos in the eBay category three times several years back. Each time he brought his books up to number one, two, and three in the eBay category. Malik held the top position for nearly a week. When he ended the promo, he returned his books to $6.99 and continued to rank high in his category.

How did he do it? I found the answer on his Amazon Author Page. When I looked at his most recent blog post, it advised readers, "99 cent sale (hurry!) – every one of my Kindle eBooks."

If you have not started to build an email list, you need to start one. Smart marketers reach out to their emails lists every day. They use them to launch new books, boost titles with sagging sales and to discover what readers want next.

To learn more about email marketing, read <u>Email Marketing Blueprint, The Ultimate Guide to Building an Email List Asset</u> by Steve Scott.

Kindle Countdown Deals

There seems to be a lot of confusion about how to best use the Kindle Countdown Deal.

Some authors do not understand how to use it. Some worry about it not being available in all areas. Others look at it as a watered-down workaround for KDP Free Days.

First, we need to understand what the Countdown Deal is. Amazon says it is a "new KDP Select benefit that lets authors provide readers with limited time discount promotions on their books. It's an opportunity to earn more royalties and increase the discoverability of your book. Customers will see the regular price and the promotional price on the book's detail page, as well as a countdown clock showing how much time remains at the promotional price. You'll also continue to earn your selected royalty rate on each sale during the promotion."

A quick read through should answer any questions about how to use Kindle Countdown Deals.

First off, it is a limited time promotion. You can set the period you want it to run – anywhere from one hour to seven days. You can also set the discount levels. If your book is $3.99, you can split the promotion over three levels. Your book starts at 99 cents. It increases by one-dollar increments divided across the promo period. The timer resets for every price level. It shows buyers how long they have left to buy your book at the discounted price.

Some of the complaints are it is too confusing. There should be one price point for the entire promo. Or, the counter is too cheesy or pushy. This ignores the whole point of the Countdown Deal. The urgency of the timer ticking away makes readers rush in to buy now, before the price moves to the next level. If you take away the timer, sales are going to nosedive. If you only want one discounted price, you have complete control over that. Choose the price increment that best suits your needs.

Some authors say they will not use it because other authors said it did not work for them. That is a shortsighted view of things. Just because it did not work for Stephen King does not mean it will not work for you. Listen to what other authors say, but do not let them make the decision for you. Try every available tool out for yourself. If it does not work, discard it. If it does work, add it to your toolbox.

Another thing that concerns some authors is the deal is not available to everyone. Martin Crosbie talked about this in an *Indies Unlimited* blog post. He said he had problems changing prices worldwide so that no one would feel left out.

Amazon decided where the deal would be available. It is an Amazon thing. Use the deal the way Amazon intended. Do not worry that some readers cannot take advantage. It is not your fault.

KDP Free days do not work for every author or every book. It all comes down to the book you are promoting. The days you are promoting it on, and whether other writers are running deals at the same time. A healthy dose of luck does not hurt, either.

Let me give you an example.

I ran my first Countdown Deal several years ago. I experimented with ten of my books. One title sold seventy-five books in the seven-day period. Another sold sixty-five copies. That was two to three times the number of books I sold the week before without running the Countdown Deal. Not too shabby. Five of my other books sold from five to fifteen copies during their seven-day run. Three of my books did not sell a single copy.

Overall, it was a good promo.

The two books with the best sales sustained their initial sales bump for almost a month. They remained among the top five sellers in their category.

The best indicator that it worked for me came from my Kindle sales and commission reports. Total Kindle sales were up 250 copies for the month. My royalties rocketed up $300 from the previous month. CreateSpace royalties shot up over

$700 for the month, but I have no way to tie those sales to the Countdown Deal.

Would I run another Countdown Deal? It is a no-brainer. Yes, I would, and I am doing it now. The two best books from my last run, *eBay Money Machine* and *eBay Unleashed* are having a good run again. One surprise seller was *Abraham Lincoln: The Baltimore Plot*. Both of my KDP Free promos failed to give away over a few hundred copies, and sales never took off. Before this promo, I sold five copies over a seven-month period. During the first three days of the Countdown Deal, it sold twenty-one copies. This may be its breakout moment.

Sales would have been higher for the eBay books, but Steve Weber ran the Countdown Deal on his books during the same period. Luck was not on my side this time. It is okay - I still had a great promo. Sales of *eBay Money Machine* remained steady for several days after the Countdown Deal ended.

Weber's Kindle Countdown Deal showed that the promo works well for bestselling books. His book Barcode Booty jumped from a 12,000 to 15,000 ranking in the Kindle Paid Store to around 1800. Three days later it still ranked around 7800. One day, three of his books ranked one, two, and three in the eBay category.

The Kindle Countdown Deal made them bestsellers, again.

Steve Scott talked about the Kindle Countdown Deal in one of his blog posts. He said a few of his books sold several hundred copies during the promo and kept going strong afterward. Some of his books did not do as well. He shared the same info about using Kindle Free Days; sometimes they work, sometimes they do not.

If you do not try it for yourself, you will never know what works best for your books.

Kindle Countdown Deals are a great promotional tool for authors. Unlike KDP Free Days, Kindle Countdown Deals can help you grab some more sales and make money too.

Keep close tabs whenever you run a promo. Decide for each book which promo is going to do a better job – Free or discounted pricing.

I recently caught up with author Rob Parnell to get his take on Countdown Deals.

"From my perspective, Countdown Deals are much better than free days. I'm often stunned by how little difference it makes to give away thousands of books – mainly because all the hype says it does so much good. Countdown Deals generate a lot of sales for me. Plus, they keep you in the chart after the deal has expired."

Martin Crosbie said he is, "seeing results utilizing Kindle Countdown Deals through KDP Select. I run a three-day promo with my book at 99¢, and I supplement the promo with an ad on E-reader News Today, Kindle Books and Tips or BookBub."

If you want to sell more books during your Countdown Deal, you need to advertise it. Anymore, when I launch a new book or run a Countdown Deal, I run promotions. That keeps the sales rolling in, especially when I spread the sales out—one a day over my promo.

Try it. You will like the results.

Kindle Unlimited

Kindle Unlimited is Amazon's answer to free reading sites. For $9.99 subscribers can read an unlimited number of books. It is a win-win for readers and authors. For readers, they can sample new authors without any risks (other than the time they invest in reading your book). Kindle Unlimited is an inexpensive way to build your fanbase without having to shell out a bunch of cash.

If you have not sampled Kindle Unlimited, it is easy to get started. Hop on over to *Kindle Unlimited* and sign up for your subscription. It is that easy. Once you sign up, you can download up to ten books at a time. If you check out more than ten books, it prompts you to return a book for every book you want to download.

Amazon reports over one million books enrolled in Kindle Unlimited. Some of the selections come from large publishers. But, most of them come from self-publishers like you and me.

Kindle Unlimited is a hot mess right now. If you write longer books (over 200 pages), you will be okay. If you write short books (25 to 100 pages) the newest change to Kindle Unlimited is going to hurt.

The payout for Kindle Unlimited reads went from roughly $1.41 per borrow to .0058 cents per page. What that means for authors is if your book is fifty pages long your royalty payout is 29 cents. If your book is 100 pages long, you get paid 58 cents in royalties.

Youch! That stings.

If you write short books, it may be time to change your strategy. Write longer books or do what I did and pull your shorter works out of KDP. Publish them on other sites.

Amazon - By Invitation Programs

You can bust your ass forever trying to turn your book into a bestseller, but the simplest and quickest way to hit a home run is to wait for Amazon to come knocking.

I have been self-publishing books on Amazon for just over five years now. I have picked up well over $100,000 dollars in royalty payouts. Several of my books have climbed into the top one-thousand books on Amazon, but after my promotions ended they took the inevitable plunge into oblivion.

In November of 2017 I received a quality control notice from Amazon. They had found some issues with my bestselling book, *Shot All to Hell*. It was an invitation to work with them to make my book the best book it could be. There was no pressure to make changes, just an offer to help.

What the hell! I jumped onboard. They suggested some simple edits and asked me to set up the X-ray feature. After a few weeks of work and some back and forth emails, I resubmitted the book.

Several weeks later, I received an invitation to enroll my book in the Prime Reading program. They offered me five-hundred dollars to give my book away to Amazon Prime members for ninety-days. My book was already enrolled in Kindle Unlimited, so why not offer it to Prime members as well?

A week later my book rocketed up the charts from a 97,000 ranking to the top eight-hundred books on Kindle. I moved from a zero ranking in history writers to as high as number thirty-one. Almost immediately, I noticed a bump in my paperback sales, and my page reads jumped from a few thousand to nearly fifty-thousand per month. My guess is I made another $500 per month from the visibility boost I received from being enrolled in Prime Reading. The only surprise was audiobooks. Sales remained flat during my entire Prime enrollment period.

Over the previous eighteen months I had spent well over $1500 promoting this book. It sold well and made money while I was promoting it, but no matter what I did, sales eventually slowed.

That was not a problem while Amazon promoted my book. Sales remained consistent for the entire period my book was enrolled in Prime Reading, and the rank remained between 800 and 2500.

Three months later, I received a notice from Amazon that the promotional period was up, and my book would be removed from Prime Reading. I would receive the agreed upon payment with my next royalty payout. At that point, my book ranking started to fall but it was okay. It was a fun ride, and I got to outsell many of my favorite authors.

My thought was that was the end of the story. Little did I know, Amazon had other plans. They sent me a notice saying, "we're excited to tell you that your book, *Shot All to Hell*, has been enrolled in a new Amazon beta program called Great On Kindle – a program for high quality nonfiction eBooks that make them easier for customers to discover."

Pretty cool, right? It was nice to know Amazon was not going to desert me just because my Prime Reading gig was up.

After that, they explained the Great On Kindle Program in more detail. "As part of Great On Kindle, we plan to experiment with things like a detail page message that helps readers discover high quality books, Amazon funded-promotions for customers, and nominations for merchandising opportunities." It also talked about special price promotions available to program members.

A few days later I received another invitation from Amazon to participate in special price promotion opportunities. Under this program, Amazon reserves the right to promote your book in various programs over a six-month period. The promotional price could be anywhere between 99 cents up to the retail price of your book. Whatever price they set for the promotion, you receive your standard royalty rate of 35% or 70%. They also opened a new royalty rate for books enrolled in the program.

Authors can now choose a 50% royalty rate. I know what you are asking yourself. Why should I settle for a smaller royalty payout? I asked myself the same question.

Here's the deal.

If you take the 50% royalty rate you can price your book between 99 cents and $20.00 and receive the 50% royalty split. If you are selling your book for 99 cents, it gives you an extra 16 cents in royalties per copy sold. If you want to price your book higher than $9.99, you can boost your royalty payout a few bucks instead of taking the 35% payout.

Another way you can benefit from the 50% royalty rate is if you have a graphics intensive book. Amazon does not charge file delivery surcharges, so it should give your royalty payout a boost.

So, when Amazon comes a knocking make sure you answer. They can market your book better than any promotion you can dream up.

FYI: If you are interested in another take on Amazon Prime Reading for authors, Steve Scott and Barrie Davenport created a podcast that detailed Steve's experience with Prime Reading. Even though Steve acknowledges a nice bump in his rankings and royalty payouts, he does have reservations on whether he would enroll another book in Prime Reading. Listen to the podcast to find out why.

Analysis of Amazon Prime Reading for Authors

Book Promotion Ideas

A lot of authors look at marketing as something sleazy or beneath them. They feel it is their job to write the book. After that, Amazon, Nook, iBooks, or whoever the publisher is should promote it.

The problem is that is not how it works. The reality is—it is up to you to promote your book.

If you do not have a ready-made audience or platform, you need to hustle. You need to help the right people find your book.

It reminds me of the girl who broke off her engagement with her long-term boyfriend. She goes out on the town with her girlfriends hoping to forget everything. The next thing you know, she gets a little tipsy and falls for some sleazebag's pickup line. I do not need to tell you the rest of the story.

What is she going to do when she wakes up in bed the next day and finds herself next to him?

Book marketing is a lot like that for many authors. We run a promotion to get that initial pop in sales, but we do not have a plan to keep our books selling over the long haul.

We look for quick fixes.

We get drunk on that first rush of sales. We get caught up in the dream that this time it is going to be different. Sales are not going to stop. Our book is going to go all the way to number one and hang out there forever.

Of course, the reality is going to kick in sooner or later when we take off our beer goggles. That is when most of us realize—book-marketing is not a one-time thing. Most often, it is a series of one-night stands.

We need to cozy up to this group and then this group. Like our tipsy young friend, scammers and sleazebags abound. They tell us—no problem. They offer to push our book to number one with no effort involved on our part. They promise we can sit back and watch them perform their magic, and oh yeah! That will be fifty. One hundred. Or, one thousand dollars.

Of course, there are no guarantees.

One morning we wake up to a slew of sales. Another day— well—it is hard to look at ourselves in the mirror.

A guy has got to try, right?

That is what this section is all about. I am going to take a deep dive into book marketing. What works? What does not work? And, why sometimes certain promos work, and sometimes they do not.

I will say it again.

There are no guarantees. A promo may work one-time and fail the next time around. Your favorite promo website may rocket one book to the top of the charts and sputter out with another book.

Here is the cold, hard truth—book marketing is situational. It is a lot like believing in Santa Claus, the Easter Bunny or the Tooth Fairy. Eventually, it comes down to faith. If you do the right things, good things are sure to follow. That is how it works. Think of your book promotions as you do about leaving milk and cookies out for Santa Claus. It is the piste de resistance—the icing on the cake.

When you do it, it leaves a warm fuzzy feeling deep inside of you.

Book Promotion 101

Promoting your book used to be so easy. You would book a date, set your price to free, and watch the downloads pour in. You could always count on 2500 to 5000 downloads for a three-day giveaway. And, you never had to spend a nickel on promotion. When the giveaway ended, you would see a nice bump in your paid sales. Often, several hundred paid sales would follow.

That was then; this is now.

Today, if you set your book to free and do not promote it, you are lucky to get 100 downloads.

WTF!

The rules of the game have changed. Every time you think you have it figured out, someone goes and changes the rules of the game—again.

The biggest challenge is determining which sites give you the biggest bang for your buck. It is not a sure thing that you will break-even. Think about that before you decide to drop three or four hundred dollars to promote your new book.

Everyone wants to feature their book on <u>BookBub.</u> But, BookBub is expensive, and they are choosy—really-choosy. To get featured on BookBub, you need a lot of high-quality reviews. You need to meet their rigid editorial standards. You need an expensive, professional cover design.

Even some of the smaller book promotion sites are getting more selective. They choose which books to promote based on how many reviews your book has and its star rating. If your book does not have a four-star or better rating—keep looking because a lot of sites will not feature it.

Too bad, they are not as exacting when it comes to producing results.

What happens when you spend $25 or $50 and only get fifty downloads or two sales? Authors should know which promotional websites pay off and which ones do not.

Maybe I am crazy, but when I plunk down my hard-earned cash for a book promo, I expect results.

To put it in sexual terms I want a happy ending!

I ran a five-day KDP Free Promo for my book **History Bytes**. It got downloaded over 5,000 times. It grabbed the number one spot in the history category for three days. And, it ranked 131 in the Kindle free store. Not my best promotion, but far from my worst.

I shook things up a bit this time.

Typically, I run one or two ads on the first day to kick off a two or three-day promotion. This time I did things a little different. I stacked my promotions so that I had at least one ad running every day.

Day one started off with features on Choosy Bookworm and The Fussy Librarian. Costs: Fussy Librarian $25.00, Choosy Bookworm $48.00. Total downloads 625.

Day two had a single promotion on Free Booksy (one of my favorite sites). The ad cost $75 and garnered 1252 downloads.

Day three featured my new favorite promotional website - Robin Reads. Cost $55.00. 2741 downloads.

Day four started with a Read Cheaply promotion. Cost $25.00. 644 downloads.

Day five ran with another favorite and inexpensive promotion by James H. Mayfield. For $13.00, James submits your book deal to as many as thirty promotional sites. It saves you a lot of legwork, and it gets results. This time, I received 181 downloads. Previous promotions with Mayfield received two or three times that number.

Looking back on it, I messed up when I scheduled my promotions. I should have run the FreeBooksy ad on day four, and the Robin Reads ad on day five. This would have shown Amazon's marketing engine that my sales were steadily increasing, not decreasing.

Live and learn, right?

After the KDP promo winds down, I expect sales to take off at a nice clip. Sometimes paid sales roll in right after the free promo ends. Other times, it can take a day or two for sales to begin rolling in.

Do not panic if it takes a little time for sales to kick in.

I planned to keep the price discounted to 99 cents for at least thirty days. Somewhere between week two and three, I ran a promotion on <u>Bargain Booksy</u>. It cost $25 in the nonfiction category. I did this six or seven months ago with another promotion of **History Bytes**. Over a three-day period, I sold 253 books.

With the Bargain Booksy Feature that brings the total cost of my promotions to $266. To break even, I need to sell 788 books at 99 cents per book.

That is a shit ton of books.

Worse yet, nothing happened. My promotion did not work out the way I hoped. I sold less than 150 eBooks, a few paperbacks, a handful of audiobooks, and got 15,000 page reads.

As promotions go, it was a disappointment.

Now for the fine print.

Your results can vary based on the books you promote and how many times you have already promoted them. The first time I promoted **History Bytes** on FreeBooksy, it received 8900 downloads. Sales blasted off after the KDP free promo ended. Ever since then most of my promos on FreeBooksy have gotten between 800 and 1200 downloads. It is not the performance I want, but the result did not come as a complete surprise either. FreeBooksy is promoting it to the same list. Each time you promote the same book to the same audience, it is going to have fewer downloads. It is the law of diminishing returns.

Book sales is a numbers game. To get the best bang for your buck you need to plan your promotions wisely.

Do not promote the same book on the same website more often than every 90 days. Every 180 days would be better. Spread your promotions out, or you risk burning readers out on your offer.

Here is another word to the wise.

Do not run a five-day promo if you are not going to promote it every day or at least every other day. Most book promotion sites email their list early in the day. By eleven o'clock sales start to roll in. You will get most of your downloads before six or seven o'clock. After that, they trickle in at a much slower rate. The day after your promotion ends downloads drop dramatically. You need to be ready with another promotion to fire things up again.

That is why ad-stacking is so important.

Ad-stacking is the new buzz word in Internet marketing. If you are unfamiliar with the term, ad-stacking is something like playing Dominoes. You run one ad after the other. That way you keep the momentum moving from ad to ad.

I like to run a mid-size promotion on day one. That primes the pump and pushes my book into the top two or three hundred books on Amazon. Most often, I hit number one in several key categories. The next day, I run a larger promotion on *FreeBooksy* or *Robin Reads*. That pushes my book up the lists. I usually score first place in my prime categories. Often, I rank among the top fifty or one hundred books in the Kindle free store.

Once you reach the number one spot in your key categories, everything else is irrelevant. It is great for your ego, but more downloads are not going to get you a lot more sales. You need to push your book into the top five books in the free store—and even then—there are no guarantees. Several of my books hit number the number three spot in the free store, then had a miserable showing when they returned to paid.

That is why I say; results are not a sure thing.

Here is what I can tell you. To make the top five list you need between fifteen to twenty-five thousand downloads. It depends on your competition that day. From what I understand, it takes fifty thousand or more downloads to hit the number one spot.

Sometimes you can get there with a whole lot of luck. Other times you can get there with some well-planned promotions and a big wad of cash. It is all about how much you want it.

Before I wrap this discussion up, I am going to mention two more promotion sites I have had good luck using.

The first one is <u>bknights</u> on Fiverr. This guy (or gal) has three gigs running with over 4,000 feedbacks total, and they deliver results. The standard price is five bucks. When the results have been so-so, they refunded my payment—even when I did not ask for it. Bknights promotes your book on their website <u>http://digitalbookspot.com/.</u> They offer gig extras that feature your book on their email list. You can submit free books and discounted books. I have had good luck with both.

Another promotional service I have had good luck with is <u>http://freebookservice.com/</u>. These guys are not cheap, but they do produce results—and they do guarantee them. They have three packages to promote your free book. They guarantee 5,000, 10,000, or 15,000 downloads. I have always done much better. With the 5,000 package, I received 8900 downloads. With the 10,000 package, I received over 13,000 downloads. With the 15,000 package, I got 23,000 downloads. That pushed my book to the number three spot in the Kindle store—three times). Prices range from $189 to $379, so it is going to cost you some money. I should also warn you these guys are provoking a lot of controversy on the Internet. Some scam warnings say they are not real downloads; others say Amazon will take your book down if you use them. That is not true. I used *Free Book Service* five times. I received the promised results and never received a threat from Amazon. If you have concerns, contact <u>Amazon customer service</u> before you make a move.

My best advice is if you have a new book, run your free promotion for five days. If your book has been out for a while, consider a two or three-day free run. Promote the hell out of it. When the promotion is over—lower your price to 99 cents for at least seven days. If you are not in it for the money keep your book at 99 cents for thirty days. You will get more paid sales and reviews.

If you do a 99-cent promotion, set up a *Kindle Count Down Deal.* Stack your promotions using *BargainBooksy, Robin Reads, bknights,* and other promotional sites. Doing this makes you 70-cents per book, compared to 35 cents. The extra 35-cents is not a lot of money, but it should help you break even a little quicker.

Another new promotional service I used was yournewbooks.com. I tried a special that promoted my book over a three-week period. It cost me something like $60. The results sucked. I would take a pass on this one for now—at least until they can grow their list and work out the kinks. My sales were miserable. I netted five sales and a limited number of free reads over the three-week period.

They should have paid me for the bother—not the other way around.

Enough said.

If you do not get the results you want, don't sweat it. Not every promotion is going to take off. Some will take you in different directions than you expected. I ran one promotion for **History Bytes** where audiobook sales took off out of the blue. I watched the book go from a ranking of 80,000 on *Audible,* all the way down to 288. For a while, I outsold Bill

O'Reilly, Stephen Ambrose and other giants in the history category.

Do not ask me why?

I do not know if it took off on its own, if Amazon promoted the hell out of it, or if some book blogger started pushing it. You cannot plan for these things. They just happen. I remember Steve Scott talked about one of his books and how it hit number one on Amazon right before Christmas. He did not have any idea what happened, but he said it was a hell of a lot of fun watching his book make its climb to the top. In the end, he figured some book blogger promoted it to his list and the rest as they say—is history.

Eventually, luck will push you to the top of the heap. Until it does, keep plugging away.

Write another book.

Retool Your Infrastructure

Is anyone else out there tired of the book promotion rigmarole? Let me tell you; it frustrates the hell out of me.

Last year I spent four or five thousand dollars to promote my books. I made some good money, but I am not sure it increased my income. Most of the books that sold went for 99 cents which means I made roughly 34 cents per copy. To break even I would need to sell 18,000 copies.

Yowch! That is a shit ton of books.

Some of my books would get a nice bump for three to five weeks after the promotion ended. Then they would go back to sleep. It became a vicious cycle. If I did not promote my books, they did not sell. That is not entirely accurate. A few sales or page reads would trickle in over the course of the month but nothing to write home to mom about.

This year I decided to shake things up a bit.

My plan is to invest in the infrastructure of my books, rather than discount them. The idea is to step my game up a notch.

My first investment was in professional-grade covers. So, I said, "Bye, bye Fiverr. Hello, 99 designs." That shot my cover costs up from five or ten bucks to two hundred dollars plus artwork.

It is scary to drop two bills on a cover, but the results are what count, right?

If you have never used *99 designs*, it is like *Fiverr* on steroids. You start a **contest** (their term for project). Within hours designers begin to submit cover designs for your inspection. Designers have four days to submit their designs. Many of them present multiple concepts. You can like the designs you receive, discard them, or ask the designer to make revisions.

What surprised me is that this all happens in real time.

The pace is fast.

Many designers chatted back and forth with me. They submitted remakes or all new concepts within an hour or less. If I had to compare it to anything, I would say it is something like "**Shake 'N Bake,** and I helped."

The first contest I submitted was for a remake of my cover for **History Bytes**. I liked the cover I had, but everyone told me it was so-so. The book sold well. It had since I released it. I just thought it could do better and if it meant redoing everything, it seemed worth giving it a shot.

I received 32 designs. I narrowed it down to six by the fourth day of the contest. If you want to know the truth—the first layout I received nailed it. Once the designer added the Confederate flag background, there was no going back.

It is a fantastic design. Sales have nearly doubled since I republished it with the new cover.

Next, I submitted **Shot All To Hell**. Again, I liked the original cover and had doubts I could do any better.

Foolish me.

I received 76 designs for **Shot All To Hell**. They all looked great, but in the end, I had to make a choice. Two designs grabbed my attention. The clipart for one was $68; the other one was $45. What can I say? I cheaped out and went for the less expensive clip art. But, I still love the design. I know it is going to sell a shitload of books, and that is what it is all about anyway, right?

I did have one relapse during this time and had another cover designed on *Fiverr*.

I did this one a little different. I dug through period magazines and located two black and white illustrations. Next, I had a designer on *Fiverr* color the drawings. After that, I made a mock-up of what I wanted with MS Paint. Then, I sent everything off to a cover designer. The first designer came close, but his design did not hit the nail on the head. So, I sent it to another designer along with copious notes that specified what I wanted him to change.

He nailed it.

After that, I went back to the drawing board and redesigned the interior of **History Bytes** and **Shot All To Hell**.

I added pictures, then found a *Fiverr* designer who could format the book. He added picture wraps, drop caps and all the goodies the professional publishers use.

I do not want to brag, but the results were mighty damn impressive.

Will the new covers and the retooling of the contents sell more books?

The answer is a resounding yes. It even scored me bonus points with Amazon. I will tell you more about that later.

Amazon Ads

I love Amazon ads.

I have been running them for a little over three months now. The one thing I can tell you is they work. More importantly, Amazon Ads work the way all book promo sites should—you pay for results.

To date, I have spent several thousand dollars on Amazon Ads. Amazon says those ads resulted in nearly $10,000 in sales.

Not bad!

If you figure I made a 70 percent profit on each sale. That is a gross profit of $7,000. Deduct the cost of the Amazon ads and I made $5,000. Try to make that profit from a KDP free run or a Kindle Countdown Deal. You cannot do it.

One of the terms you are going to hear when you talk about Amazon Ads is your ACOS—short for Amazon Cost of

Sales. To find the ACOS you divide your sales ($10,000) by the ad cost ($2300). That number is your ACOS.

So, in this case, my Amazon Cost of Sales was 23.01 percent. Or, to put it in simpler terms, for every quarter I spend, I make a dollar.

It is like playing the slots. Only you are a guaranteed winner. I like those odds.

In theory, if I want to be a 5-figure author, I would need to run $2,500 in ads every month. That would give me $10,500 in sales with a $7,619 gross profit.

It sounds good, right?

The thing is, it is hard to get Amazon to spend your money. I can tell it to spend $25 a day, and it spends $1.25.

WTF!

Mark Dawson is an expert on Amazon ads and he says the same thing. To get the spend thru he wants and needs, Mark runs over 200 ads at a time. Two-hundred ads is not going to happen.

I run twenty-five ads at a time, and to me it is a lot of work.

If you have not tried Amazon Ads yet, here is how to get started.

Go to your seller bookshelf. Select promote and advertise. On the next page, choose Create an ad campaign. Or, if you prefer to go directly to the Amazon ads interface, click on the Reports tab in KDP. On the next page, select Ad Campaigns.

The page that pops up next is your campaign dashboard.

To promote your book, select New Campaign. If you are asked to sign in, enter your Amazon id and password.

Two boxes pop up. One is for Sponsored Products. The other is for Product Display Ads.

Sponsored Product Ads display below the Customers Who Bought This Also Bought section in product listings. You can target them with keywords you select, or you can let Amazon auto-target prospects.

Product Display ads appear on product detail pages. They also display on the Kindle screensaver and home screen. You can target books by genre or products related to your book.

Most authors do not use Product Display ads. They have a minimum $100 buy in, and the reporting is not as straightforward.

Product Display ads give you two ways to target your audience. You can choose by product or interest. If you choose by product, Amazon shows "your ad on Amazon.com to customers interested in selected and similar products." If you choose by interest, your ad shows on "Kindle E-readers and Amazon.com to customers interested in selected categories."

In the next section, you target the products and books relevant to your title. Choose as many similar books as possible. This ensures your book gets shown to the maximum number of interested readers.

You can also target by interest or category rather than choosing individual titles or authors. It is easy, but in many cases, a one size fits all approach is not as effective. If you choose "biography," it targets all biographies, not just the ones related to your book. Because of that you may end up paying for unrelated clicks.

My best advice is to try Product Display Ads, but do not bet the farm on them. Concentrate most of your budget on Sponsored Product Ads.

To set up a sponsored Products ad, tap on the box. Next, you select a book to advertise. You can choose it by title or by ASIN. Tap on select by the title you want to promote.

After this, pick a campaign name, budget, and duration. I go with the campaign name Amazon suggests. Whatever you do, include a title, date, and a few words about what you are targeting. Next, set your daily budget. Five or ten dollars should be fine, but you can go as low as one dollar. The truth is, it is next to impossible to spend over two dollars a day.

Once you set your budget, set the ad duration. You can select a "date range," or "continuously." Do yourself a favor and select continuously. My bestselling promotion was set for a limited period because I was unsure what to expect. When it ended, I copied the promotion and ran it again. Unfortunately, I could not replicate the results.

After you set the duration, select a "Targeting Type." The choices are automatic and manual.

Automatic "targets your ads to all relevant customer searches based on your product information." Manual targeting is "based on the keywords you choose."

After you make your choice, select a cost-per-click bid. Amazon suggests 25 cents. You can choose any amount, even as low as a penny. Go with the quarter to start. In most cases you are going to spend much less. Amazon runs silent auctions for each term. The higher your bid, the better your ad placement. You want to be on the first page or two of sponsored ads, but do not go spend crazy. If you overspend, it is going to make it tough to make a profit.

If you chose Automatic Targeting, the next step is to create your ad. Amazon gives you 150 characters. Shorter is better.

Here are three of my ads.

- Does it seem like your cell phone is taking over your life? Here's why.
- Life was cheap in the old west. A marshal's star served as an invitation to drunken fools, gunfighter wannabes, and men seeking a reputation.
- Think you know history? This book will force you to rethink everything you know about American history.

As you can see, Amazon does not give you a whole lot of room not much room to tell your story. Throw out a teaser. If it does not work after a few weeks, try another one.

Now, we are going to setup a sponsored ad.

> Tap on the Sponsored Products box.

> Select the book you want to advertise.

> Name your campaign.

> Set a daily ad budget. $2.00 to $5.00 should do it. It will be a while before you can get Amazon to spend that much. Select a duration.

> Do yourself a favor and choose run campaign continuously. You can always shut it down later if you prefer.

> Select a targeting type. You have two choices—automatic or manual. Choose manual.

> The next step lets you select your bid per keyword. Amazon suggests 25¢. Go with that. Whenever I bid a quarter, I usually end up spending 5¢ to 15¢. Sometimes I get the bid for a penny.

> After you set your bid per click, it is time to choose your keywords. Amazon makes suggestions based on your book. Select the ones you want to keep and discard the rest. You can have up to a thousand keywords. I would recommend at least 200 to run a successful campaign.

Choosing your keywords is not rocket science, but it does take a lot of hard-work. Pull up the categories your book is listed in and start coping and pasting the titles and authors into a spreadsheet.

Some experts suggest skipping best-selling authors or titles. I am not so sure about that. Some best-selling books or authors are duds for keywords, but you will not know for sure until you give them a try. Give your ad a week or two to do its magic. Check which keywords are performing, and which ones are not. Delete or pause the keywords that show a poor ROI.

Targeting keywords is really that simple.

Target as many competing books and authors as you can. Sprinkle in a good portion of search terms related to your title. Stir, or monitor often. That is all it takes.

> After you add your keywords, it is time to write your ad copy. Keep it simple. You only have 150 characters to work with, so don't try to write a novel.

- Tease your readers.
- Ask a provocative question.
- Challenge potential readers.
- Use the words "you" and "yours."
- Make it all about them.

As you write your ad, Amazon shows you what it will look like. Give it a once over to make sure you do not have any typos, then click submit.

In 24 – 48 hours your ad will go live.

Monitor your campaigns weekly. Pause or delete the keywords that are not working. If you find a keyword making great sales at a 5% or 10% ACOS, consider doubling down and raising your bid.

If a keyword performs extremely well, make it one of your seven keywords in the KDP dashboard. If it works for Amazon ads, it should boost your organic sales as well.

While you are at it, recheck your book description. Sprinkle in your bestselling keywords from your Amazon ads campaign.

Amazon Ads (Part II)

Bryan Cohen ran an amazing tutorial a while back about how to scale up your Amazon Ads.

If you have ever used Amazon Ads, you know how hard it is to get them to spend your budget. You can set a five-hundred-dollar budget, and they will spend fifty bucks.

Wtf!

It is an uphill battle. The more money you throw at them, the less they spend.

Don't believe me? Revise your budget to $250 or $500. Most times your impressions will not budge.

Bryan put an interesting spin on things.

First off, he shared his view that half the battle is waiting for Amazon to start spending your money. Too many authors give up after three to five weeks because their ads have not taken off.

Cohen thinks that is a big mistake.

He thinks authors should take the long view.

The real magic does not happen until your ads have been running for four to six weeks, sometimes much longer. You need to give the Amazon Elves enough time to sprinkle their magic fairy dust.

It is frustrating. Especially if you are impatient, and demand immediate results.

It is not going to happen overnight.

If you are willing to wait. I can guarantee you good things will happen.

Here is the good news!

Amazon Ads work.

They can make you a lot of money. I spent $287 over a two-month period and made $1498 in sales. That does not include Kindle page reads, audio books, or paperbacks.

So, no matter what you think, Amazon Ads can be an author's best friend. You just need to have a little patience and be willing to tweak your campaigns.

Where I disagree with Bryan is in his definition of a successful campaign.

He suggests that we are looking at the wrong metrics. He says you should concentrate on overall dollar sales. If you are making money, your Amazon Cost of Sales (ACOS) does not matter.

Some of the examples he showed made me shake my head. He had an ACOS of 100 to 300 percent or more!

That is a lot of red ink.

Cohen's justification was he is getting a big return on Kindle page reads which are not included in your ACOS score.

Cohen shared that the ads are helping him launch a new series, and to date he has received over a half million page reads. If he includes that money in his sales calculation, the numbers look much better.

I agree with that.

Before I started running Amazon Ads, I rarely sold paperback copies of my history books. Now I sell twenty-five to thirty copies a month. The royalties from paperbacks alone almost cover the cost of my Amazon Ads.

That makes the payoff much more substantial.

If you have not used Amazon Ads, you need to give them a try. If you are currently using Amazon Ads, and you are not getting the result you want, you need to shake things up a bit.

- Run more ads
- Include more keywords
- Test different ad copy
- Give your ads more time

Finally, I think, it comes down to the books you promote. My history books are a natural for Amazon Ads. They draw a lot of attention. My business books are mostly dogs. They make decent sales on Amazon, but Amazon Ads do not drive sales to them.

Do your homework. Experiment. And, make more money.

Here is one more tip. Read <u>Mastering Amazon Ads</u> by Bryan D. Meeks. It is an enjoyable and enlightening read that takes a deep dive into Amazon Ads and how to make the most out of them.

Let me warn you up front. The process is not easy, and it involves math. (I do not know about you, but that scares the bejeezus out of me. I hate math. I go out of my way to avoid it.)

With that said, I think most readers will employ the basic advice Meeks gives to supercharge their ads. I also think most readers will ignore the tracking portion of the book.

That is a shame!

But, it is math. And, like I said earlier. That is some scary stuff! Did I tell you? I do not like math. I do not like to think about it. I do not like to do it.

Enough said.

Here is the gist of the book.

You need to run a boatload of ads, and you need to constantly monitor their progress.

Just when you think you are running all the ads you need, you need to post more.

Amazon Ads have a shelf life. Some ads last for a few hours or a few days. Other ads can run for weeks, or even months.

Your mission, should you choose to accept it, is to determine when your ads are going to stop running, and have new ones ready to take their place.

Hint!

This is where math comes into the equation.

Meeks says you need to track when your ads start and stop for each of your books. Once you know your numbers, you can be proactive and have new ads ready to go as soon as the old ones stop performing.

There is more tracking you need to do, such as your cost per click, the number of clicks that turn into sales, and your ROI. The thing is, all of that involves math, so I am going to refer you to the book for that information.

BookBub Ads

BookBub has got to be one of the most frustrating book promotion sites to work with. Their turndown notices state they accept fewer than twenty percent of the deals that get submitted.

I am zero for five. So that should mean my next submission is a sure thing. Right?

I am not so sure about that.

I am pretty sure they put my name on the auto turn down list. You know, they do not say no forever. Instead, they ask you to please not contact them for at least thirty days. But, I am pretty sure they have a secret file of authors they will never accept.

And, my guess is, my name is at the top of that list. At least it sure feels that way.

Now, there is some good news for BookBub's forgotten few.

They have created a workaround where you can still promote your books on their website. The only catch is you are relegated to a display ad at the bottom of the page. One that never opens on my iPhone. (I hope BookBub is working on this.)

Anyway, BookBub began testing author ads in May of 2016. Right now, authors need to submit a request to join the program. I think it took four to six weeks for them to determine my money was the right color of green.

The program itself is easy to use, and it does work. You will get clicks, and you will start making sales the day your ads begin to run.

Just be warned. It is expensive. And, it is next to impossible to break even.

So far, I have invested $250, sold fifty books at $3.99, and earned about $140 worth of royalties. That is roughly a 55 percent return on my investment. Maybe, I got a couple of hundred page reads that were not tracked. That would bring my earnings up to $160.

That is nowhere near the result I was hoping for. But, when I look online at other author's results, it seems I did not do half bad.

Some authors I read about said a twenty to forty percent return is the about best you can expect. Others said it was okay to break even because dollar sales do not factor in page reads. Maybe they got more page reads than me; I do not know.

Enough whining!

BookBub tells you up front, "although BookBub Ads appear in regular BookBub daily emails, they are completely separate from Featured Deals."

The good news is you can feature your books at regular price, a temporary discount, or as part of a KDP Free Promo.

Pricing is entirely up to you.

I think if I were to do it again, I would coordinate my BookBub Ads with a Kindle Countdown Deal at 99 cents or $1.99. That leaves a little extra meat on the bone to pay for the promotion. The last time, I ran my promotion over three days, and sales picked up immediately. I sold four books with the first ten dollars, so I decided to double down, and jumped my budget another $35.

That was my first mistake.

Or, maybe it was my second mistake.

My first mistake was probably using BookBub's ad editor. It is a clunky beast that kicks out a really poor-quality ad. It featured my book cover and some nasty looking black text.

Remember what they say about not being able to judge a book by its cover. It is easy to judge it by the quality of your ad. That was my first faux pau.

Needless to say, I was sure I could do better. I plunked down fifteen bucks on Fiverr and had three new ads designed. They all performed about the same. The funny thing is, the crappy ad I created with the BookBub editor performed the best. I am not sure if it was a fluke, or what. I will update this section after I do more testing.

Like I said, earlier - enough whining.

Here is how to get started once you get the go ahead from BookBub.

Click on this link to see BookBub's tutorial.

https://insights.bookbub.com/category/bookbub-ads/

When you are ready to post your first ad, click here.

https://partners.bookbub.com/ads

If you are creating your first ad, you need to click on the green GET STARTED button in the upper right-hand corner of the screen. If you already have an ad running, the DASHBOARD displays the stats for the ads you are running.

I ran four ads over a three-day period. I cut all of them off, except for the two ads for History Bytes. My total ad spend was $46.22. I received 15,182 impressions and 148 clicks. My average CPM was $3.04 for an average CTR of .97 percent.

I know, right off, you are probably thinking what the hell does that mean?

For those of you who use Amazon or Facebook ads, you know those services charge per click (you pay every time someone clicks on your ad). BookBub chose to switch things up a bit. They charge per one-thousand impressions or CPM (in human speak, that means you pay for every one-thousand-times they show your ad. Clicks are not charged separately).

In other words, you place a bid, based on how much you are willing to pay for them to display your ad one-thousand times.

Now that you understand how the program works, here is how to create your first ad.

1. CHOOSE YOUR BOOK. Just like it sounds. Type in the title of your book.

2. CREATE YOUR AD. You can use the BookBub Ad editor, or you can upload your own image (recommended). My suggestion is to pick several Fiverr designers and have them create a 300 x 250 banner ad.

3. Enter your CLICK-THROUGH LINKS. The cool thing here is that you are not limited to just Amazon. If your book is available on CreateSpace, Audible, B & N, GoogleBooks, or iBooks you can add those links, too.

4. This is the hard part. You need to target your audience. It is a two-step process. First, you REFINE BY AUTHOR. It is easier than it sounds. You pick out authors of books like yours. Next, you REFINE BY BOOK CATEGORY. Again, it is easier than it sounds. Pick categories that fit your genre.

5. You can target by author or category, but BookBub says you get better results if you use both. When you do this, you pick up readers who enjoy both the author and the category. To make it simple, the more interested readers you target, the better your chances to make more sales.

6. SCHEDULE AND BUDGET. You can set your ad to run continuously or to run over a set period. Unless you are running a limited time price promo, I would suggest that you choose to run your ad continuously. Next, you set a budget. It can be as little as a dollar, or the sky is the limit. You choose. If you normally run Amazon ads, this is an entirely different ballgame. BookBub will spend the entire budget you set. It is nothing like Amazon where you can set a $50 budget and spend five bucks. So, make sure you have the money to spend before you set a limit.

7. Now it is time to set your BID. On BookBub you bid per 1,000 impressions or CPM. They say the higher your bid, the more bidders you will reach. The suggested bid is $7.44 to $12.44 per CPM. In most cases, you will pay less. I bid $5 to $7 per CPM, and my average spend was $3.04. If you are just starting out, I would bid $5 or less. Your ad will display, and you can test your return on investment (ROI) before you go all out.

8. The last step is to NAME YOUR AD. Make it simple. Use the name of your book, the date, and the keywords or the market you are targeting. This makes it easier to dissect your campaign later to determine which ads worked and which didn't.

That is pretty much it. After you press continue, your ad goes into a short-review period before it starts running.

The wait is nothing like Amazon. My ads were up and running within an hour and I made my first sale not much later.

If you have not tried BookBub ads, I would give them a shot. I am not sure they will make you rich, but if you want to get some quick sales or focus a lot of eyes on your book over a short period, BookBub ads are the ticket.

Social Media

The talk among authors is you cannot strike it big without a significant social media presence.

I am not sure whether that is true or not. I look at social media as another trick you hold in your toolbox. It can help build your author brand. It can help you sell more books. But before any of that can happen you need to develop a plan.

Without a plan, social media can become a major time suck. It keeps many authors from doing what is most important – writing another book.

Success with social media is not about posting to Facebook every half hour. It does not have anything to do with sending out tweets. You need to build a connection with your readers. You need to make them come back for more. If you are lucky, they may check out a few of your books.

So how do you do that? Stress quality over quantity. Research shows that the most shared posts are images or short videos. What this tells you is if you want to get more likes you need to post short image-oriented items.

Make a funny face while you point at a headline in a newspaper or magazine. If you are traveling, post a bunch of selfies of yourself standing by local monuments or statues. Photoshop yourself next to President Obama, Captain Kirk, or a literary hero. Insert one of those bubble captions with a quote from one of your books. Use some crazy thought that just popped into your head.

Make it fun! Make it worth checking back every day to see what is next. Develop a reputation for presenting strange news, crazy facts, or telling it like it is.

Every time I tell my kids something stupid, I say "interesting dinosaur factoid #____." Naming my stupidity helps to build the conversation. They look forward to hearing what comes next. So, will your followers.

With a little modification, I could translate that to Facebook. I could have a little dinosaur dude drawn up with the words "interesting dinosaur factoid." I could insert the number in my post. If I did it enough, people would check back to find out what crazy thing I am going to say next.

What about you? You do not have to do anything crazy, or stupid.

If you write about history post a simple factoid about "today in history" or "this week in history." Grab a piece of clipart or a public domain image. Slap up some juicy tidbits of history your readers might be unfamiliar with.

If fiction is your thing, write a Facebook novel. Post short 100 or 200-word chapters every few days. If you write historical thrillers, post pictures that match your content. Think European castles, knights on horseback, and damsels in distress. Grab YouTube clips from Renaissance Festivals and post them to your timeline.

There are all sorts of interesting things that your fans would like to know more about.

The more useful the information you post, the more likely it is readers will keep checking back. They are going to want to know what comes next.

If you want to be successful with social media—give more than you get. Aim to entertain and educate your fans. After you have earned the right, you can mention your free book or Kindle Countdown Deal. Follow it up with more information your followers can use.

Explaining how to use the individual social media sites is beyond the range of this book.

The big players at this writing are Facebook, Twitter, LinkedIn, Pinterest and Instagram. Some authors like to establish a presence on every site. My suggestion is to select one or two that interest you. Set aside a half an hour or an hour a week to build your brand. One or two posts per week should get the ball rolling.

How to Revive A Dead Book

It is natural for book sales to slow down over time. It is just the way it works.

Summer is a slow time for book sales – period. If your book sales slowdown between May and August, you should shrug your shoulders and let it go. Run a Countdown Deal or feature your book at 99¢ for a few days every month to keep your sales going. If things do not pick up by September, then you may want to attempt more drastic methods to revive your book.

After a while, Amazon shakes up categories and begins featuring newer books. They do not want their inventory to get stale. Amazon knows that readers prefer newer books. If you are willing to do a little work, you can make this change work for you. The trick is to bring out a new edition of your book. Revise your book. Add extra information. Write a new introduction that summarizes updates in the field. Add pictures, charts or expert interviews.

If you write fiction, open your bag of tricks. Add extra content to your book. Append an alternate ending. Provide a character outline. Include additional chapters that bring more depth to one of your minor characters.

After you make your changes, update your book cover. Write a new description that reflects your new and revised content. In the KDP dashboard list this version of your book as the second edition. Change the publication date so that it reflects the time of your revision. In effect, you are releasing a new book without all the extra work.

The following case study talks about how I revised and rebranded several of my eBay guides.

Case Study

What do you do when the subject you write about is constantly changing?

Do you sidestep the issues of pricing, fees, and changing policies? Do you concentrate on the basics because you are afraid to give specific advice that will date your book? Do you dive head first into the fray? Do you give specifics when you know the information changes every six months or year?

That was the dilemma I found myself in several years ago. Most of my eBay guides were becoming dated. They still sold well and ranked in the top ten or twenty books in their category. But, I noticed a lot of new books published in my niche. They did the same thing. They danced around the issue of fees and policy updates.

I gave it a lot of thought. Many of my reviews said readers wanted to know more about what it costs to sell on eBay. They wanted to know how eBay's new and changing policies affected their business. They wanted to know what the changes meant for them going forward.

I revised four of my books. I rewrote at least twenty percent of each book. I added a new introduction and had new covers designed for each of them. I rebranded one of the books. I gave it a new title, changed the contents around, and rewrote significant portions of it.

That one went on to become my bestselling book, *eBay 2015*.

Another one of my books worried me.

eBay Unleashed always sold well. I rebranded it with a new cover and made minor changes to the contents to reflect eBay's new policies. The first two months after the new edition came out sales dropped twenty-five percent. I do not know how many times I wanted to roll all the revisions back—but I did not. From hindsight, I can look back and be glad I waited it out. Sales bounced back. It is a consistent money-maker bringing in $500 to $700 per month in royalties.

I do not think any of them would be selling this well if I had not taken the chance and revised them.

How else can you resuscitate a dead book? Often, a few minor changes can help you sell more books. The trick to increasing sales is to track your sales and determine when sales first started to drop off. Sometimes, it can mean a competing book entered your niche. Readers might be buying it rather than your book. If this is the case, you need to examine that book and determine why it is selling better.

Does it have a better title? Is the description more enticing? Is the content more up-to-date than yours?

Be honest with yourself. If the problem is a new book in your category, the best thing to do might be to do nothing. Over the last three years, I have watched dozens of new books jump ahead of mine in the eBay category. Most of them run their course in a month or less, then slip back down the charts. If the problem is more persistent, check out the book descriptions. Sometimes tweaking your synopsis can make your book seem more attractive to readers.

Other times, your price might be the problem. When I first started selling my books on Kindle, I priced them at $4.87. As the eBay category became more congested, I dropped my prices to $2.99 to remain competitive. Some authors in my category began slugging it out. They priced their books at 99¢ hoping to reach the number one spot on the charts. I decided to stay out of that battle and let them give their books away for nothing. I did not want to be a bestseller that bad.

Sometimes it may be the opposite problem. If your price is too low, readers are going to ask themselves why? They are going to wonder what's wrong with your book. Try raising the price a few dollars. That might be all it takes to get your sales going again.

Change your title or cover. Here is another trick big publisher's use.

Have several versions of your cover made up when you publish your book. Run the first cover for two weeks. If sales are not what you expect, switch your covers out—it is possible a different cover may sell more books. Sometimes different background colors can increase sales. Other time a different cover can boost lagging book sales.

The same thing goes for your title. A bad title can keep your book from selling. I named one of my books *My eBay Sales Suck: How to really make money selling on eBay.* It did ok. Most months it sold sixty to one hundred copies, but I always thought it could do better. I changed the title *to eBay 2014: Why you're not selling anything on eBay and what you can do about it.* Since I made that change, it has sold closer to two hundred copies every month.

Key Takeaway: If your book is not selling, it is up to you to revive it. Strap on your thinking cap. Step up your marketing.

Goodreads Giveaways

One of the Catch 22's for authors is you need reviews to sell more copies of your books, but to get more reviews you need more readers.

Because reviews are so critical to a book's success authors have resorted to all sorts of tricks to get them. Some authors have bought reviews on Fiverr (a no-no that can get your book booted off Amazon). Other authors have joined Facebook groups that encouraged members to buy each other's books and leave favorable reviews. Just understand, if Amazon discovers what you are doing, they will delete those reviews.

The old standby is to ask mom and dad, brother and sister, and all your friends to leave reviews. The problem is Amazon frowns on reviews from friends and relatives and will take them down if they discover the connection.

So, if you cannot buy reviews and you cannot ask friends and family to review your books, what can you do?

Some authors take time out to write Amazon's top-reviewers and beg for reviews. Sometimes it works. Most often, it does not, because thousands of other authors are following the same playbook.

Other authors bombard their mailing list with free offers, then encourage takers to leave reviews. This is probably the most effective method of getting reviews. It is also the safest method for getting them, because the odds are the people on your mailing list know and like your work and will likely leave a thoughtful review.

I am not above asking my mailing list to write a review in return for a free copy of my book. In the past, I have written top-reviewers to solicit reviews, but the payoff has been negligible.

The most successful method I have used to get reviews is Goodreads Giveaways.

They have recently changed the program up and started charging users a hefty fee to give away your books. I gotta admit when I saw it cost $119, or $599 to give away a copy of my book I began to have doubts about the program. In the past, Goodreads Giveaways were free to list your book, but you had to pay to purchase copies of your book and mail them out. Depending on how many copies you chose to give away, that could easily run one hundred dollars or more.

Looked at that way, $119 is not so bad.

Here are the details of the program. The base charge is $119. For that, Goodreads will advertise your giveaway and distribute up to one-hundred copies of your Kindle book. How many copies you choose to give away is up to you. It can be anywhere between one and one-hundred copies. Why you would give away less than one-hundred copies of your book does not make sense to me because the more copies you give away, the more reviews you should receive— in theory, anyway.

I am just trying out the new model now. When I mailed out physical copies of my book, 25 to 40 percent of winners left written reviews. A few more were lazy and just left star reviews. They all help, right?

My hope is I can get a minimum of eight to ten written reviews, and another ten to twenty-five-star reviews. If I hit that goal, Goodreads Giveaways will become my go-to marketing program for every new book I release.

The $599 program lets authors give away paperback books, or up to one-hundred Kindle books. The choice is yours. The other difference is if you pay the larger fee, Goodreads will promote your giveaway in more places and on their home page.

If you have a big new release, the more expensive program could pay off by giving you more exposure on Goodreads. For me, one-hundred readers signed up for the giveaway the first day, so more promotion sounds like overkill, or throwing good money after bad.

If you give away print copies of your book you can autograph them, and include a handwritten note asking for a review. That could easily double the number of reviews you receive.

No matter which program you choose, Goodreads contacts winners eight weeks after the contests ends and reminds them to rate your book and leave a written review.

Choosy Bookworm has a similar program. They call it their Read and Review Program.

When readers request a copy of your book, Choosy Bookworm sends them a Mobi or PDF file. If for some reason you do not receive the minimum number of reviews, they will promote your book for another nine months. Sorry! No refunds allowed.

The program guarantees you will receive from twelve to twenty-five reviews within thirty to ninety days. The cost is $149 to give away thirty copies of your book, or $299 to give away fifty copies. The downside is these are not considered Amazon verified purchases, so some people will give less weight to them.

I have not tried the program, so I cannot share any personal results at this time.

Kindle Scout

<u>Kindle Scout</u> is a fan powered publishing platform for original books new to Kindle. I would consider it a hybrid somewhere between self-publishing and traditional publishing.

The way it works is authors submit their manuscripts to Kindle Scout. Amazon publishes the first five-thousand words of your manuscript on the Kindle Scout website. Readers can check out your book, and if it meets the cut, they can nominate in for publication.

That is when the magic begins.

If your book is chosen for publication, you receive a $1500 advance and your eBook will be published by the Kindle Press (Amazon's publishing arm). Upon publication your book is enrolled in KDP Select and made available for Kindle Unlimited reading. Authors receive a fifty-percent royalty, less than Amazon's seventy-percent royalty payout for a book priced over $2.99. The trade-off is you have the power of Amazon marketing your book, so you should sell more copies.

Books submitted to Kindle Scout must be all new, never published before, and a minimum of 50,000 words in length. Kindle Scout campaigns run for thirty days, so authors receive timely feedback on their books. Reader input is important in that it helps Amazon know which books are popular, but the final decision on which books get published is made by Amazon, not readers.

Several promotional websites have popped up to help authors promote their Kindle Scout campaigns. Here are a few of the best.

- **Just Kindle Books.** https://www.justkindlebooks.com/kindle-scout-promotion/. For $33.00 they guarantee to get your book into the *Hot and Trending* section for at least one day if your book is in the mystery or romance category. They offer optional Facebook promotions at an added cost.

- **Lincoln Cole.** https://www.lincolncole.net/services/kindle-scout-book-promotion. Lincoln Cole offers Kindle Scout promotional programs ranging in price from $8.00 to 32.00. The eight-dollar program gets your book listed in their newsletter. The more expensive services offer several levels of social media advertising.

- **Author Shout.** https://authorshout.com/promote-with-us/. Author Shout's Kindle Scout nomination programs run between $10.00 and $25.00. The more expensive packages offer promotional banners, and a 20 second book teaser video.

- **Huge Orange.** https://hugeorange.com/kindle-scout-promotion/. This one is pricier than the others, and starts at $100.00. A quick review shows the program is currently on hold because Amazon recently stopped allowing promotional sites to use Twitter to market their giveaways.

So, is it worth it?

When you submit your book, you make it exclusive to Amazon for 45 days. That gives them time to set up your Scout campaign, give away copies, and tabulate results. Before the end of that period, Amazon gives you a yes or a no. Traditional publishers can easily keep your book tied up for six months to a year while they piddle around deciding whether they want to publish it or not. Then they take another 18 to 24 months getting your book ready and bringing it to market. Kindle Scout will have your book published and begin promoting it to interested readers within 60 days, sometimes less.

The other big advantage of submitting your book to Kindle Scout is you have the power of Amazon behind your book. That means you will have verified reviews from day one. Amazon emails copies out to everyone who nominated your book and encourages them to leave a review. Some authors whine and complain that they only receive a 50%

royalty, not the standard 70% deal most KDP authors receive. Get over it! A traditional publisher would pay you less than 10% royalties and leave the marketing up to you. When you sign with Amazon, they do all the marketing for you. You do not have to shell out money for promotions, or for prepublication copies to send out to advance reviewers.

The power of Amazon means one more thing. They are going to do everything they can to make sure your book sells. It is like I said earlier, when my book got into the Prime Reading program it went from obscurity to broad daylight. Sales and page reads skyrocketed overnight, and my author ranking shot through the roof. That helped readers find my other books, so I got more sales from my backlist.

If you write fiction, a Kindle Scout promotion may be your ticket to the big time. Read the author submission guidelines.

https://kindlescout.amazon.com/agreement

Publishing Beyond Amazon

Kindle, Print, or Audio, which format is more important to your success?

It seems to me a lot of Kindle authors are doing it all wrong. They have this tenacious focus on eBooks and believe that print is dead.

The truth is anything but that. Yes. A lot of people have moved on to the new devices. They would not dream of serving all their new books up on anything but an e-reader. The thing is there are still a lot of people out there who like to read their books old style. They enjoy the feel of a book in their hands. They want to highlight their favorite passages. They want to make notes in the margin. They love to fold the corners to mark their favorite pages. Some people like it both ways. They like the feel of a book in their hands for those lazy days around the house. They load up their devices for when they are on the go. Amazon recognized this with their <u>Kindle Match-Book</u> program. It lets readers pick up free, or discounted eBooks when they buy the print version.

What authors need to understand is readers appreciate a choice. How did that old candy bar jingle put it, "Sometimes you feel like a nut, sometimes you don't."

Camille Picott in her book, *Indie Publishing Essentials*, touches on this same subject. She tries to make all her books available in print, eBook, and audio format. Picott says she never knows how readers are going to want her book served up. She writes that many months her audiobooks outsell the Kindle and print editions.

How about you? If your books are only available on Kindle, how many dollars are you missing out on in lost royalties? How many book sales are you losing out on because you are not offering readers a choice?

Most of my books are available as eBooks, paperbacks, and audiobooks.

My Kindle books outsell print copies by a margin of two or three to one. But, my book royalties from CreateSpace exceed my Kindle royalties.

Authors, here is my question for you. How many dollars are you leaving on the table, if you are not making your books available in print?

List your book on Kindle

Before you list your book on Kindle, you need to set up your account.

If you already have an Amazon account, you can sign in with it. Otherwise, choose sign-up and follow the directions provided. They're quick and painless.

After you sign into your KDP account, you should see four headers across the top of the page. Bookshelf, Reports, Community, and KDP Select. To get started with your book scroll part way down the page until you see add a new title. Click on it, and you will be ready to set up your Kindle book.

Publishing your book to Kindle is painless—and free. If you ever find yourself in need of help, click on the blue <why?> Link by each step. Amazon will explain what you need to do.

The blue box at the top of the screen gives you the opportunity to enroll in KDP Select. KDP Select lets authors make their book available for free for five days in a 90-day period. Amazon Prime members can borrow one free book every month. Enrolling in KDP Select makes your book available to these readers. Each time someone borrows your book you receive a piece of the KDP Select fund set aside for authors. The current payout is averaging approximately .0058 cents per page read. To enroll your book in the program, you need to make your book exclusive to Amazon for ninety days.

The next two sections ask you to provide your book title and subtitle. If your book is part of a series, put a check in the next box, and enter your series title. When you do this, Amazon ties the books together. It includes the series title along with your book title in search results. Edition number is optional. Most times I type in first edition and update this for any revisions I make. If you are self-published, you can leave the publisher line blank. If you establish a custom imprint to sell your books, you could add the publisher name here.

You have 4,000 characters to describe your book. That works out to somewhere between 600 to 800 words. I cover descriptions in more detail in the section titled Amazon Book Optimization. The least you need to know is your description needs to entice readers to buy your book. Give them a compelling reason to click on the buy button.

You can dress your book description up using HTML. Here are some of the HTML codes Amazon currently supports.

- <b> bold </b>

-
 creates a line break or space. To leave a blank space between lines, you would use the code twice

- <h1> to <h6> to create bold headings. Use <h1> to create a large headline. (Many books still say <h2> creates the large bold headline in Amazon Orange. It has not worked since the summer of 2015.)
- <hr> _____ </hr> creates a rule to divide sections of your description
- <i> formats your text in italic </i>
- <li> creates a list. You would use <ol> around each item to create a numbered list </ol>. To make a list set off with bullet points you would use <ul> </ul>

For a complete list of HTML codes supported in Amazon book descriptions, click this link. https://kdp.amazon.com/help?topicId=A377RPHW6ZG4D8

When you use HTML code, every command needs an opening and closing code. For example, <b> begins formatting the text in bold. To stop formatting text in bold, you need to close the code with the following line </b>. Using the / in the brackets tells it to stop formatting in that style.

Book contributors lets you enter the author, co-author, illustrator, and editor. The default language is English if you are publishing in the United States. Change it if necessary. The publication date prepopulates, so you can leave it blank. If you revise your book, you can modify the date, so your book shows a more recent publication date. Readers buy the most current books because they want the most up-to-date information.

Where it asks for an ISBN most often you will leave this blank and Amazon will supply an identifier for you. If you purchased an ISBN, enter it here.

During step 2 it asks you to verify publishing rights. If your book is in the public domain, select this option. If you hold the copyright to your book, choose this is not a public domain work.

FYI: If you are publishing a public domain work it is not eligible for KDP Select.

Step 3 helps you target customers for your book. The first step is to add categories. Amazon has over 4,000 categories to choose from. When you list your book, you need to select two categories. Click on add categories and choose the ones that best match your book. Over time, Amazon will slot your book in the categories it feels best suit your book.

The next section lets you add seven search words or keywords to help readers find your book. I cover how to locate keywords more in the section on Amazon Book Optimization. The very least you need to know is - keywords are terms readers use to search for your book on Amazon. Do not include your title or your name; Amazon will already search by these. You are not allowed to use other book titles or author names. Doing this violates Amazon's Terms of Service and can get your account suspended. If you want readers to know you write like Steven King, or that your book is reminiscent of Forrest Gump, mention it in your book description, not here.

Some self-publishing experts tell you to use "Kindle Unlimited" as a keyword. Do not do it! It violates Amazon's TCs. They will make you change it, or they may take your book down.

Section 4 is where you upload your cover or create a cover using Amazon's cover creator. To upload a cover file from your computer, select browse for an image to locate the file.

Section 5 lets you upload your book file. You need to select your DRM (Digital Rights Management) settings. These determine whether readers will be able to copy and loan files of your book after they buy it. The only stipulation is once your book gets published you can't change the DRM settings.

Section 6 allows you to preview your book. When you select this, you can see what your published book will look like on the Kindle Fire, iPad, and iPhone. **FYI**: A manuscript that looks perfect in word, can look entirely different when you read it on an e-reader. Look at every page using the previewer. Check for page breaks, pages that do not display the entire text, and gaps where you have several extra lines. Look for anything else out of the ordinary. Correct the most common formatting errors before you press the publish button.

There is a box below this labeled download previewer. I always use the Send to Kindle App to read my book on my Kindle Fire, and iPhone. When you read the book the way most of your readers will it makes it easier to catch errors and correct them.

After you complete these steps, select Save and Continue, to move to the next page. Or, if you're not ready to go to the next section, select Save as Draft to save your information for later.

Section 7 lets you verify your publishing rights. Most times, authors select worldwide rights. If you only hold publishing rights in certain areas, select those territories. Choose the areas that apply.

Section 8 is where you select your royalties. If the selling price of your book is less than $2.99, or over $9.99 you should choose the 35% royalty option. If the sale price of your book is between $2.99 and $9.99 you should choose the 70% royalty. After you choose the royalty rate, you need to enter your list price. After you enter the list price, it displays the delivery charge and estimated royalty.

FYI: If you selected the 70% royalty rate Amazon charges you a delivery fee based on the size of your file. The larger your file, the higher your delivery charge. (If you're worried about delivery charges, use as few illustrations and charts as possible. Be sure to compress all your files before embedding them in your manuscript.)

Check the box to base all your prices on the United States price. Or, you can set the prices for individual territories. The fine print explains how the VAT tax applies in Europe and Great Britain.

Section 9 lets you enroll your book in the Kindle MatchBook program. MatchBook lets readers who buy the paperback get the eBook for a discounted price. Even if you set your MatchBook price to 99¢, Amazon pays you the 70 percent royalty rate.

Step 10 enrolls your book in Kindle Book Lending. This let's book buyers lend their book to a friend or family member for fourteen days one time. By default, all books making a 70% royalty get enrolled in the lending program. You can opt out of the lending program if your book is earning a 35% royalty.

After you complete everything, you need to accept Amazon's terms and conditions. Then select save and publish. Your book should be for sale within twelve to forty-eight hours, usually sooner.

Anytime you want to make changes; you can come back to your Bookshelf and make changes.

Amazon recently added the ability to publish paperback books directly from the KDP dashboard.

Rather that break it down step by step, I am going to say it is intuitive and follows the Kindle set up process. If you are used to publishing your paperback books on CreateSpace, give the KDP dashboard a chance with one of your next books. It is much easier to use than CreateSpace, and you do not have to wait twelve to twenty-four hours for it to generate a proof. It is displayed on the spot, and once you approve it, your book is published.

CreateSpace paperbacks

CreateSpace is an Amazon company. They give authors a low-cost option to produce paperback versions of their books.

Getting started with CreateSpace is easy. The first step is to determine the trim size for your book. The suggested trim size for trade paperbacks on CreateSpace is 6 inches x 9 inches. Choosing this size ensures that your books sell through the most outlets possible. CreateSpace lets you choose from 15 different trim sizes.

After you chose a trim size, you need to format your manuscript. The easiest way to format your CreateSpace book is to use MS Word.

First off, you need to choose a font. I have had good luck using Times New Roman and Calibri. Many professionals recommend Garamond or Book Antiqua. Format a chapter of your book using each font and decide which one you like best.

After this, you to need to set your page margins. Before you start, make a duplicate copy of your manuscript and work on it. This way if something goes wrong you can recover from it. Go to Page Layout – Size – More paper sizes. Select the page size you want. I set my margins to 0.50 all around. If you have a larger book, you may want to adjust this to fit more text on each page. CreateSpace charges based on how many pages are in your book. The fewer pages you use, the cheaper it is to print your book.

Now, you need to number your pages. Go to Insert – Page Number and select the style of page numbers you want to use. I like to use Bottom of Page – Accent Bar 1 because I can include the book title at the bottom of every page.

Choose your line spacing and paragraph indents. Most nonfiction books use block spacing with a line between paragraphs. Works of fiction often use paragraph indents with no space between paragraphs. I use paragraph indents and a line between paragraphs when I format my books. It gives them a better look. There are no hard and fast rules. If you have a large book, use paragraph indents with no space between paragraphs. It will save on printing costs.

If your book contains images, ensure they are high-resolution images (300 DPI). Low-resolution images can sometimes appear blurry or grainy. CreateSpace will single them out later in the proofing process.

This provides you with a good basic manuscript you can upload to CreateSpace. It will pass their automated system check. If you want a more professional look, hire a professional to format your book. They will ensure your front and back matter are professionally formatted. If you are a do-it-yourselfer, read this book. *Self-Publishing: How to Publish like a Pro for a Fraction of the Cost* by Donna Joy Usher.

Getting Started

Before you list books on CreateSpace, you need to register. Go to https://www.createspace.com/ and select Sign up.

Log into your account, click on add new book. In the Start your new project box, type in the name of your project. Select paperback. Where it says, choose a setup process, select guided (especially if this is your first book). Press get started to move to the next screen.

Fill out the necessary information – title, author, and contributors. If you are unsure how to answer any questions, click on *what's this* and it will give you directions. At the bottom of the page, click save and continue.

Next, you need to choose an ISBN. You have four choices. Most authors have CreateSpace assign a free ISBN for their book. You can buy a custom ISBN from CreateSpace for ten dollars. If you have a custom imprint, this is an inexpensive way to add a more professional look to your book. You can buy a custom universal ISBN from CreateSpace for $99. This gives you more options than the generic ISBN. The difference is you can use the custom universal ISBN with other publishers. The regular ISBN only works with CreateSpace. The final option is to provide your ISBN. You can buy them through Bowker or from online discounters.

Depending on the type of ISBN you buy it can limit your distribution options. All the ISBNs work with expanded distribution. To sell to libraries and educational institutions you need a CreateSpace assigned ISBN.

Select the option you want and follow the prompts. Click on assign ISBN to move to the next section. The next page shows your ten digit and thirteen-digit ISBN. A message pops up to say your ISBN is locked. You cannot change it later. If you want to change the title or author, you need to assign your book a new ISBN.

Click on continue.

This section lets you select the trim size and interior of your book. The default trim size is 6 inches x 9 inches. If your book is another size, select choose a different size and pick the size you want to use. After this, you need to choose an interior type – black and white or colored pages. Choose your page style – cream or white. Cream pages resemble the look of a traditional book.

In the next section, you upload your book file. Choose upload your book file, and it prompts you to select a file. They accept manuscripts in these file formats--.pdf, .doc, .docx, and .rtf. You can talk with someone from CreateSpace about professional design services. Costs start at $199 depending on the amount of formatting involved.

While you wait for the interior file to upload, you can start working on your cover. Otherwise, it takes a few minutes to process. When the automated print check finishes, it lets you know if there are any errors. Click on launch interior reviewer to proof the contents of your book. It lets you page through your book to see what the final print will look like. If everything appears ok, click on continue.

This section lets you work on your cover. The first thing you need to do is select a finish for your cover – matte or glossy. Matte is a dull finish. Glossy is bright and shiny. For my money, the matte finish makes a better-looking book. After you select your cover type, choose how you want to submit your cover design.

You have three options.

1. Use the CreateSpace, cover creator.
2. Hire a professional cover designer from CreateSpace (starting at $399).
3. Upload a PDF ready cover.

I am not going to go into details on how to use the CreateSpace, cover designer. Some of the styles are nice. It all comes down to whether you want to put a generic cover on your book or give it a more professional appearance.

My suggestion is to hire a professional designer. Several designers on Fiverr do a good job and will format your cover for ten to twenty dollars. Two of them I have had good luck working with are –

http://www.fiverr.com/rroxx/create-awesome-professional-ebook-cover-design

http://www.fiverr.com/vikncharlie/design-you-an-awesome-book-cover

If you upload a book cover select browse to choose your file, then click on save. The next page shows that your cover uploaded successfully. It also gives you the option to make changes. If you are happy with what you have, click on continue.

Next, submit your book for review. Before you submit your files, it gives you an option to edit files. If everything is okay, select submit files for review. A pop-up box says your files are being checked. Click on continue to choose your distribution options.

Your books get listed for sale on Amazon.com, Amazon Europe, and the CreateSpace e-store. Royalties are larger when you sell through the CreateSpace e-store. Whenever possible link to it when selling copies of your book.

The next section displays the expanded distribution options.

Selecting Bookstores and Online Retailers makes your book available through online retailers. Within a few days, your books become available at Barnes & Noble, Books A Million, eBay and others. You earn less when books sell through expanded distribution, but you sell more copies. In my case, I make between $250 and $300 per month from expanded distribution sales.

To sell to schools and libraries choose the Libraries and Academic institutions option. CreateSpace Direct makes your books available through independent bookstores and retailers. Your book isn't likely to appear on store shelves, but if customers request it, a bookstore can order a copy for them.

After you select your distribution channels, click on save and continue.

CreateSpace shows the smallest price you can charge (you must charge at least this much for each book). Before you set your price, play with the pricing tool to see what you earn at different price points. If you selected expanded distribution, make sure you will not lose money if you price your book too low. From what I understand CreateSpace will deduct any losses from your royalties.

If you write fiction, price it somewhere between $7.95 and $12.95. Base it on what other books in your genre sell for. If you sell nonfiction, you should be able to command a higher price. I charge $15.99 for most of my eBay guidebooks. One of them sells a consistent one hundred copies per month. Several others sell twenty-five to fifty copies per month. I have seen other authors stretch their price to $19.99 or $25.99. You can change your prices at any time.

After you price your book, click on save and continue.

The last step is to post your book description, categories, author bio and such. You can use up to 4,000 characters in your synopsis. Use basic HTML to enhance your description. To add a space between paragraphs you need to add the <br> code to add one line. To add two lines between paragraphs, use

.

You are only allowed to choose one category so pick the one that best defines your book. Under additional information, you can add your author bio. I copy and paste it from my Amazon Author page. Be sure to use HTML code to dress it up. Add the <br> code to add spacing between lines and paragraphs. Under search keywords, you can enter five search terms. It limits you to twenty-five characters. When you finish this section, click on save and continue.

You need to wait twelve to twenty-four hours for Amazon to check your files. When CreateSpace completes their automated file check, they email you with the results. If everything is ok, you need to proof your book. You can use the online proofer, download a PDF proof, or order a physical proof of your book.

Once you approve the proof, your book goes live on Amazon. Most times, Amazon associates your print book with your eBook. If they do not, email customer service and they will get that taken care of for you.

After you finish creating your book you have the option to have your book formatted and sold on Kindle. I have never used this option, so I cannot tell you exactly how it works.

CreateSpace has made it possible for me to make a living writing. My royalties per book are two to three times what I make when I sell a Kindle book. And, the best news is they pay royalties thirty days after you earn them.

FYI: Most times Amazon will discount your books for a few bucks to keep sales rolling in. Even when they discount your book, Amazon pays you royalties based on the full retail price.

It works the same way if another retailer drops their price and Amazon lowers their price to match them. I had this happen with one of my books. The regular price was $12.99. Barnes & Noble dropped their price to $7.99, and Amazon matched it. I still received $5.62 in royalties per copy. The only exception was on copies sold through expanded distribution. My royalties for those sales paid out at a $7.99 retail.

If you do not have a paperback version of your book, get one made.

Audible Audio Books (ACX)

ACX is an Amazon company that sells books in the audiobook format. They make audiobooks available on Audible, Amazon, and iTunes.

The least you need to know is audiobooks are still an emerging market. Amazon has twenty-five million plus titles; Audible only has 200,000 audiobooks available. Over the next five years, that number should grow to over one million audiobooks. That puts audiobooks in the same position Kindle was in three or four years ago. They are a growth market. There is plenty of opportunity for good books, producers, and narrators.

Getting started on ACX is easy for authors.

Visit *ACX.com*. Midway down the page, an address bar asks you to enter your ISBN, book title or author name. After you do this ACX displays your book or a list of your books.

To get started click on This is my book tab; it takes you to the next step in the process.

Choose how you want to make your book available. The choices are:

1. I am looking for someone to narrate and produce my audiobook.
2. I have this book in audio, and I want to sell it.
3. I will narrate my book and upload it later.

The first option is what most authors should select. It will help you to find a qualified narrator to read and produce your book. When you choose this option, ACX shows their book posting agreement. Read it over and click Agree & Continue.

On the next page, you need to fill in some general information about your book and your ideal narrator. The book description prepopulates with information from your Amazon book page. Where it asks for copyright information, you are the copyright owner of the book and the audiobook. Fill this information in along with the year of copyright.

Next, select if your book is fiction or nonfiction. Then choose the category that best describes your book.

Below that, it asks questions about the ideal narrator's voice. Be as specific as possible when you fill this section out. It will save you from listening to a lot of auditions that miss the mark.

Use the additional comments section to list more information about your book. Explain what you are looking for in a narrator. When I listed my books, I talked about their ranking on Amazon. I said how many books I sold, and how I promoted them. Producers told me this information helped them decide if the project would pay off for them or not.

A few of my books only sell a few copies a month in Kindle or paperback. I told producers that and explained the books were short and easy to produce. I did not lie or hide the facts. Producers appreciated my honesty. All eighteen of my projects got snapped up within a few days of listing them.

The last step on this page is to upload your audition script. You can upload a file or link to a URL where you have the audition script located. ACX does not give you a character length to use as a guideline, but 4,000 characters are probably okay. I upload three to five pages of text. The audition lets you hear how the final book will sound.

After you upload your sample, click ok at the bottom of the page. It directs you to the final page of information ACX needs to collect.

At the top of this page, it asks how many words are in your book. ACX estimates how many hours your final production will be. (Hint: It is roughly 9500 words per hour).

Where it asks for territory rights, select the regions covered by your copyright. The default response is the world. If you only hold rights for one country or region list that location instead.

The next section lets you choose how you want to pay for your production. There are two choices:

1. Royalty share. The narrator/producer covers the cost of production and does all the work associated with it. When the audiobook goes up for sale, you split royalties 50/50 with them. ACX handles all the details and pays each of you. Your only responsibility is to upload a book cover (2500 x 2500 pixels).
2. Pay for production. You pay a narrator/producer to make the audiobook for you. In return, you receive all royalties earned from sales of your audiobook. If you choose this option, enter the amount you will pay per hour of finished audio. The going rate is $200 to $400 per finished hour. I have seen some producers offer to work for as little as $50 per hour. Others list their rates at $500 or more per finished hour.

After you select your payment method, it prompts you to choose the type of distribution you want. If you select royalty share, the only option is exclusive distribution. Your audiobooks get listed on Audible, Amazon, and iTunes. Your royalty is 40%, and it gets split 50/50 between you and the producer.

If you paid someone to produce your audiobook, you could choose non-exclusive distribution. This lets you sell through Audible, Amazon, iTunes, and other methods of your choice. Your royalty this way is 25%, and you keep it all.

After you make these selections, click Save & Continue to move to the final page. This page summarizes your information. It gives you the option to post your book's information to ACX.

If you already have the book on audio and want to distribute it through ACX, chose the second option. "I have this book in audio and want to sell it." Follow the prompts to list your book through ACX. Select the territory you have rights for. Select exclusive distribution through ACX (40% royalty), or non-exclusive (25% royalty). On the next page, you need to agree to ACX's terms of service. On the last page, you provide information about your book and post it for sale.

The last option is to record your audio and upload your book yourself. If you choose to do this, ACX offers several tips on how to do the best job possible. You may also want to check out How to Create an Audiobook for Audible by Rob Archangel and Buck Flogging. They explain the process in more detail and talk about the equipment you need to make a good recording.

The Author's Guide to Audiobook Creation by Richard Rieman is another excellent reference book if you are just getting started with audiobooks. Richard produced nine of my audiobooks and I can vouch for the quality of his work.

My experience with ACX has been fantastic. Their interface is easy to use. They prompt you to include the proper information every step of the way, so it is unlikely you will mess anything up. Within hours of posting my books, I received dozens of auditions. Many of them came from producers with years of experience narrating eBooks. My first four books were ready and up for sale in less than three weeks. The first week my audiobooks went up for sale we sold fifty-eight copies.

The key to getting good results is to listen to each of your auditions carefully. Ask yourself if the narrator's voice and tone match your book. Most often I know within the first ten seconds if the narrator is a good fit for my book. Trust your gut. If it sounds good to you, it will sound good to other listeners.

If you have doubts about a narrator, pass on the audition. There are plenty of producers and narrators looking for viable projects. Given time, they will find your books.

Final thought. I listed eighteen audiobooks for production in the same week. I went with the royalty share option. It saved me money up front and allowed me to get all the projects going at once. If I had it to do again, I would cherry pick my books and pay someone to produce my bestsellers. Over the long haul, I would make thousands of dollars more in royalties.

Babelcube

Most authors receive some international sales. About fifteen percent of my book sales come from the United Kingdom. Other countries account for another one to two percent of my sales.

Babelcube lets you increase sales by offering translations of your books. They provide translations in Spanish, French, German, Portuguese, Japanese and Chinese.

To check out Babelcube follow this link http://www.babelcube.com/.

Babelcube connects writers with translators. It is easy to use. Upload your book information and wait for translators to contact you. For authors, there are no upfront costs. Babelcube handles all the details. They split the profits between you and the translator, and of course, they keep a small cut for the house.

Commissions vary based on how much revenue your books take in. Babelcube takes 15% for brokering the deal. Your split ranges from 30% to 75% depending on how many copies your book sells, and the revenue generated. You receive 30% of revenues for sales under $2,000, and 75% for sales over $8,000. Like Kindle, they pay sixty days after sales get made. One caveat, your payment needs to be $10.00 or higher to receive payment for the month. To view the complete royalty schedule, follow this link. *http://www.babelcube.com/faq/revenue-share*.

Within twelve hours of posting my books, I inked deals to have five of my eBay books translated into Spanish.

My thought is Babelcube is a great concept. They recently updated their user interface, but it is still hard to use. I had a translator skip on three of my translations. To their credit, Babelcube did cancel the translations when I asked them to.

With that said, Babelcube has not worked for me. Most months I receive a $10 or $20 royalty payment. On my best months, I get $40 or $50. The best I can say is I have not made a bunch of money on Babelcube, but I have not lost money either. It has been more of a wash.

To get started you need to sign up at http://www.babelcube.com/register/.

At the top of your home page, there are four tabs – profile, books, translations, and messages.

When you click on Profile, it asks you to provide your contact information. Fill in as much as you can. I posted my

Amazon author bio, my picture, and included links to my website.

When you click on the Books section, it gives you the option to Add Books. Follow the prompts and add your book details. I copied my book description and most of the other information from my Amazon book page. You can add one book or your entire catalog.

The Translations tab shows what offers you have received. Click on the book title and scroll down to the bottom of the page to get more information about your projects. It displays the translations in progress and the translators handling the project. At the bottom of the page, there are three tabs – edit book, upload book material, and return.

Edit book lets you change your description or upload a new cover. Upload material enables you to upload your book file. You should also upload the book description and your author biography. The translator should translate these when they prepare the book. When you press Return, it takes you back to your profile page.

The Messages tab holds your correspondence. Use it to send messages to your translators.

The one thing I will say for Babelcube is they offer excellent customer service. They are quick to respond to inquiries.

Create a paperback translation

Babelcube added print books for your foreign translations in 2015.

They made it simple to use. You do not need to know anything about publishing, formatting, or book layout to publish your paperback. Follow Babelcube's four easy steps.

To get started, go to your Translations page. It is changed now to include a box labeled Paperbacks. Click on Paperbacks. It takes you to the first step of creating your new book.

When you click on Paperbacks, the following box appears. It's titled Book File. You have the option of using the interior file that Babelcube generated for your book or to upload one of your own.

You can view the file created by Babelcube by clicking the blue link labeled here. When you do this, it downloads a PDF file of your book's content. Babelcube does all the work for you. They formatted the text, added page numbers, and headers with your name and the title. I did a quick look through all my books, and the page breaks are excellent.

My problem is the trim size they chose. Babelcube's standard paperback is 5 x 8, rather than the 6 x 9 size for a trade paperback. It is not a big deal, and if most of the books they publish are fiction, it makes sense because most novels are 5 x 8.

At the bottom of this page, choose whether you want to use Babelcube's book file or your own.

The next section is Book Properties. It lets you choose the page and cover styles for your book. Page style is a personal preference—white or cream. I prefer cream because it looks more like a regular book. If you want a more professional look or have many illustrations, white pages may be a better choice.

Next, choose whether you would like a matte or glossy cover. What that means is a dull finish (matte) or a shiny finish (glossy). My personal preference is matte. Dark colors look better with it. The other key takeaway from this page is the book size - 5 x 8 inches.

Step 3 is for you to upload your Book Cover.

If you have not formatted a paperback book before, this can be the trickiest step. The cover gets sized based on the number of pages and the page style. When done correctly, the cover wraps around the pages for a perfect fit. If you want the book title and your name on the spine, your book needs to be roughly 123 pages. If it does not have that many pages, leave the spine blank.

I recommend that you have a cover designer format the cover. That way you know you have a great looking layout.

I have my covers made by a designer on Fiverr.

It is simple, inexpensive, and sized right every time. I send the designer the front cover design, the back-cover text, and a few notes about the size and formatting. I give them the book size (5 x 8), the number of pages, and the page style

Writable: Self-Publishing Simplified

(white or cream). The designer takes it from there and turns it into a publishable cover.

If you prefer to do it yourself, Babelcube has a template you can download to help size and design your cover.

The last step is to set your Book Price.

This step shows you the cost of printing your book and the minimum price to charge. The cool thing is - when you enter the price, your expected royalty displays below the price box. This way you can see how much you will make at different prices points.

After you set the price, click Final Step: Publish Paperback. The presses will start whirling.

Turning your book into a paperback is that easy. Visit Babelcube today and give it a shot.

Smashwords

I have a love-hate affair with Smashwords. Here is the link to visit their website - *https://www.smashwords.com/.*

I am happy to get my books on all the sites they support. For the life of me, I cannot figure out how to configure a manuscript to get it through their "meatgrinder." The good news is I do not have to. I found a guy on Fiverr who does all the work for five bucks. His Fiverr id is Bookaholic, and he does the job in three days or less. If you want to check out his gig, here is the link

http://www.fiverr.com/bookaholic/format-your-ebook-for-smashwords-to-pass-autovetter.

Here is the least you need to know about Smashwords. They are a third-party aggregator. They post content on their website and other eBook sites. Some of the sites they make your books available on include: Amazon, Apple, Baker &

Taylor, Blio, Baker-Taylor Axis 360, Barnes & Noble, Flipkart, Kobo, Page Foundry, Scribd, and Library Direct.

The big three are Apple, Kobo, and Barnes & Noble.

Apple is the toughest nut to crack because you need to use their eBook authoring software.

Publishing your book

Smashwords does all the heavy lifting for you. When you submit a manuscript, it gets run through their "meatgrinder." It converts your document into the formats they need to publish your book on other sites. To do this, they have very specific guidelines your manuscript needs to follow.

For the sake of my sanity and this book, I am not going to cover their exact requirements. I suggest using the Fiverr gig by Bookaholic. If you go it on your own, check out the Smashwords Style Guide by Mark Coker. You can get your free copy here.

http://www.smashwords.com/books/view/52.

Your cover art may also need some minor tweaking to work with Smashwords. Your cover needs to be at least 1400 pixels wide with a height greater than the width. You can resize your cover using paint or ask your designer to redo it for you.

Once you have your manuscript and cover ready publishing on Smashwords is easy. Click on publish in the author dashboard. Most everything is self-explanatory. The pricing and sampling section is different than on Amazon. You have the option to make your book permafree on Smashwords. To do this select make my book free. Authors do this when they want to make their book permafree on Amazon or other eBook sites. You also have the option to let my readers determine the price. If you feel lucky, give this one a try. Readers can pay whatever they think your book is worth. If you use this option, Barnes and Noble will not publish your book if you submit it through Smashwords. The final option charges a specific price for your book.

The section immediately after this lets you set up sampling. Amazon sets sample or the look inside feature to ten percent. Smashwords allows you to select the sample size for your book. Twenty percent is the default setting. They suggest fifteen percent for full-size books and thirty percent of short stories. Choose the preview amount you feel comfortable giving away.

Section 5 lets you select the eBook formats to make your book available in. By default, it selects all five formats. My suggestion is to leave it like that. When you finish select yes, I agree in Section 8 and Smashwords will begin to process your book.

After you select yes, your book goes into a queue to start processing. When it finishes processing, you receive an email that says your book passed the vetting process. If your book had errors, correct them and resubmit your manuscript.

As soon as you receive the congratulations message, your book goes on sale on Smashwords. It goes into a review for premium distribution. After the review, your book goes up for sale on other sites like Apple, Kobo, and Scribd. Most often it takes a week to review your book and get it set up for premium distribution. You can check the progress in your dashboard. The second to the last column at the far right of each book summary shows the premium status. Once your book gets accepted, it will show premium approved and the date of approval. If there is an issue getting approved, you can see the error code in the next column – retailer tickets. As soon as you correct the error resubmit your book.

Selecting distribution channels

After you submit your book, you need to select your distribution channels. To do this, select channel manager in the box labeled Marketing & Distribution Tools. When you click the channel manager, it explains the royalty payout on different sites. To select your sales channels, scroll further down the page until you see your first book cover. Smashwords show the various channels available. Choose the channels you want to list your books on.

I list my books on Amazon and Barnes & Noble myself, so I opt out of those channels. This way I receive the maximum royalty for those sites. Other authors prefer the convenience of doing everything through Smashwords.

It can take from one to four weeks for your books to start selling on those sites.

Five years ago, I would have said publish your book on Amazon, then use Smashwords to distribute it everywhere else. Anymore, I use Draft2Digital. They are easy to use. They accept your books in standard formats—Word, Mobi, and e-pub. And, they are continually innovating and adding new features such as paperbacks and their own audiobook program to challenge Audible.

Draft2Digital is the new Smashwords.

Draft2Digital

It used to be, if you wanted to publish your books off Amazon you would put your books on Smashwords. Not anymore.

Draft2Digital is the new Smashwords. You do not need to put your manuscript through a meatgrinder to make it work. And, the dashboard is intuitive and easy to use.

I am going to give it a run through, so you can start listing your books—now.

When you open Draft2Digital, there is a menu across the top of the page. Your choices include: My Reports, My Account, Support, and My Books. Just below that it says Add New Book.

Tap on Add New Book to get started.

The interface is painless and easy to use. Upload your manuscript file. Add your basic book information. Enter your book description in a WYSIWYG format. It lets you bold, highlight, and underline text. If you write under a pen name, it is easy to add a new author name in Contributors box. If you have a publisher imprint, add it under Publisher. In the BISAC Subjects box you can add keywords. D2D lets you add up to five keywords, but they caution you that most publishers only use the first one or two keywords. Put your top keywords first. You can also add up to five search terms. To make it easy, use the same search terms that you would on Amazon.

Press Save and Continue.

At the top of the next page, upload your book cover. Below this, D2D displays your chapter titles. Make sure they are correct, then press Save and Continue.

The next page lets you preview your book layout in several different formats—Mobi, ePub, and PDF. Take time to download each of them and make sure everything looks good.

If everything is okay, mark the checkbox. Then press next at the bottom of the page.

The last step is to set your prices. First, you set the United States price. Below that, there is a box labeled Manage Territorial Prices. It opens a new box where you can change prices by region. Set your prices and click Change prices.

When you are done setting prices, choose the digital stores you want to publish your book to. Current choices include: Barnes & Noble, iBooks, Toltino, KOBO, Inktera, Scribd, Playster, and 24 Symbols.

The My Reports Tabs gives you a quick overview of which books are selling and how much you have earned. Charts lets you look at which books or pen names are selling. You can look at sales by day, month, or year.

My Mailing Lists adds an email sign up form to all your books. Set it up once, press the button, and D2D includes the info in all your books. Each time you release a new book, D2D sends an email notification to readers.

Statements gives you access to your sales and royalty data. If you need a sales report from two years ago, you can access it there. If you forgot to download a 1099, tap the Tax Forms Download tab to obtain printable copies.

Support is what it says. It gives you contact info about how to reach Draft2Digital.

My Books shows all the books you added to Draft2Digital. If you need to edit a book, tap on the title.

Draft2Digital pays out royalties monthly. The payment threshold is $25 for checks, and $10 for direct deposit. And, they do withhold a 15 percent cut for the house.

Overall, Draft2Digital is the easiest way to get your books set up at multiple digital retailers. The most important store is Apple.

It is so much easier than trying to get a book through the Smashwords Meatgrinder.

Lulu

Lulu is like Amazon.

It is a self-publishing platform and a marketplace for eBooks and physical books. Authors have the choice of uploading eBooks, paperbacks, or hardback books. You can make them available only on Lulu or on other platforms.

I use Lulu because they offer an easy and inexpensive way to make your book available in hardback.

My plan was to use the hardbound books as a premium giveaway for a Kickstarter campaign. In the meantime, I made six of my books available in hardback. When you select globalREACH distribution, your books are available through online bookstores.

The real problem when you publish a hardbound book is the price.

My bestselling book is *History Bytes*. It has 200 pages. If I price it at $49.95, my royalties are $10.11. If I price it at $39.99, my royalties are $6.11. If I set it at Lulu's absolute minimum price of $24.68, I don't make any royalties. If I sell the book for $49.95 on Lulu, I make $27.97—not too shabby. I can also offer different discounts to buyers who buy the book on Lulu. For example, if I provide a 20 percent discount, the book would sell for $39.95, and my royalty would be $17.97. That is still not too bad if I could make any sales on Lulu. But, that has never happened—in over three years.

The same book in paperback on Amazon sells for $15.99 and brings me a royalty of $7.33.

So, why publish your book in hardback if you are not doing it for money? Personal satisfaction was a driving force for me to release my books in a hardbound edition. I am old school. Readers from my generation didn't consider a book to be a real book unless it came in a hardbound edition. When I was a kid, I grabbed my favorite books in the book club edition. If I could not get it there, I waited for the paperback.

Lulu offers print-on-demand hardcover books at prices any author can afford. You can buy one copy or hundreds. I purchased proof copies of my books for $13.00 to $15.00 each plus shipping. At this price, most authors can afford to buy a copy for mom and dad, and close friends. Maybe, you can afford a few extra copies to impress reviewers. I even considered ordering five or ten additional copies to send to

Amazon to sell through their FBA program. I could price them at $35.00 each and still make a little over $10.00 a copy.

Publishing Your Book on Lulu

Lulu has an option on the front page of their website labeled *publish books for free*. Select it to get started making your book.

After this, it shows the different formats you can produce your book in. It also displays the sample cost and royalties for each type of book. Once you decide on the book you want to create, choose *Make Book* or *Make eBook* at the bottom of the page.

Next, select the type of book you want to make. Click on book type.

The next screen collects basic information about your book. It asks for the title, author, and distribution methods. (You can make it available to the world or just yourself. The choice is yours.) After this, you choose an ISBN. My suggestion is to select a free ISBN from Lulu. Otherwise, you can add an ISBN you already own or proceed without an ISBN. If you assign an ISBN to your book be sure to write it down. To distribute your book through resellers, the ISBN needs to be on the copyright page. If you do this incorrectly, you need to reformat the book and order another sample.

After this, upload your book files.

If you had your book formatted for a 6 x 9 CreateSpace paperback, you could upload the same file to Lulu. It will have the proper formatting for their regular hardbound and paperback books. If your book is improperly formatted, you need to redo it. Make it easy on yourself. Create an MS Word file or hire someone on Fiverr to format it for you. Lulu has professional formatting options, but they will cost you more than a Fiverr gig.

Lulu accepts your book in many different formats including PDF, Doc, Docx, and others. After you upload it, you need to select *Make Print-Ready File* on the next page. This creates the file Lulu will use to make your book. You should preview it to check for formatting errors.

When you are happy with your book file, select *Save and Continue.* Next, you create the dust jacket for your book.

If you want a basic dust jacket, you can design it yourself using Lulu's book cover creator. Pictures get uploaded in the tray on the right-hand side of the page. After that, drag and drop them into the appropriate spaces on your dust jacket. To add text, click on the white text tabs and type in your blurbs.

To get a more professional design, hire a designer on Fiverr or 99designs.

The next page lets you preview your cover. When you are happy with it, select *Make Print-Ready Cover* at the bottom of the page.

When you finish creating your book cover, Lulu asks you to describe your project. First, select a category. You can only pick one, so choose the most appropriate category for your book. Next, you add keywords readers will search for on Lulu to find your book. Separate each keyword phrase with a comma. Your description needs to be between 50 and 1,000 characters. If you copy it from Amazon, you may need to edit it down some. The remaining fields are self-explanatory— language, copyright info, license, edition, and publisher. The only field that could be tricky is license. If you are in doubt, choose *Standard Copyright License.*

Now, set your price. Play around with it a little until you find the right price. It shows how much you make at each price point if your book sells on Lulu or with global reach distribution. You can also set a discount for sales on Lulu. Doing this lowers your royalties but can make your books more attractive to buyers.

The last step is to review the information you entered for your book. Everything gets presented on a review page. To change something, select edit, then make your changes. If everything looks good, give the go-ahead to publish your book.

At this point, your book is for sale to buyers on Lulu.

To make your book available through global reach you need to jump through a few more hurdles. First, you need to buy a sample copy of the book. After you receive your sample, return to your My Projects page to approve it. If you make any changes to your book, you need to order another proof and accept it.

Sales wise, there is not much I can tell you. I have made about five-hundred bucks over the last two years selling on Lulu. But remember, most of the books I created are hardbound editions that retail for $49.95 each. The story might be different if I produced lower priced paperback books or eBooks.

Experiment for yourself to decide if a hardbound edition is on tap for one of your books. And, if you are like me— there is something about being able to hand someone a hardbound copy of your book. It is more substantial. It is a symbol that you have made it. You are a writer!

Google Play & Google Books

*[**Author's note:** Google Books is currently closed to new self-publishers. I have kept the information here in case they should allow new authors to participate again.]*

Google Play and Google Books offer another option for authors to sell their books.

Google Books is the world's largest repository of out-of-print and current books. Readers can search through millions of books to find what they are looking for. Google Books shows them the pages in your book that contain the search terms they requested. Everyday readers, researchers, and authors search Google Books to answer their research questions.

Listing your book on Google Books can expose it to an entirely different audience.

Google Play is Google's version of Kindle or the iStore. They deliver books to readers who use their Android-based platform. You can check out Google Play here https://play.google.com/store.

Getting started

To get started listing your books, go to *https://play.google.com/books/publish/.* Sign up for the Google Partners Program.

At the top of the browser page, it says Google Play in the upper left corner. Below that you will see four tabs – Book

Catalog, Analytics & Reports, Payment Center, and Account Settings

Book Catalog is where you add new books. Select the Add Books tab, and follow the prompts. A pop-up screen asks for a book identifier (ISBN). Type in your book's ISBN. If it does not have an ISBN, click on the box below that. Click ok, and it takes you to the next screen.

If Google locates your book, it prepopulates the information. If Google does not find your book, you need to fill in the information. Where it asks for a biographical note, I paste my Amazon author bio. Below that is a section labeled subjects. Use it to add categories for your book. Age groups target different demographics your book will appeal to. If the description does not prepopulate, copy and paste it from Amazon. When you finish, click on save at the top of the page.

Click on Google Play Settings in the left-hand column. The first thing you need to do is add a new price. Click on Add a new price. Type in the currency your book is priced in (For example US Dollars is USD). In the next box, type in the price (example 3.99). Finally, choose the location for that price. To make it easy, use "World." If you have different prices for different areas, you need to add each of them separately. Follow through the rest of the prompts on this page. If you are unsure what to do, hover your mouse over the question mark. It guides you through answering everything. Click on save.

Click on Google Book Settings in the left-hand column. The first question asks you to select the percentage of your book you want to sample to readers. Twenty percent is the default. You can choose another preview amount from twenty to one hundred percent. If the book is available on your website fill in the buy link text and buy link, otherwise leave these lines blank. The publisher link is the link to your publisher website if you have one, otherwise, leave this line blank. You can also upload a publisher logo if desired. Click on save at the top of the page.

Click on Content Files in the left-hand column. You need to upload your book files in PDF or e-pub formats. The cover image needs to be in JPEG format. At the bottom of this page, you have the option to upload a list of Quality Reviewers. To add someone as a quality reviewer, they need to have a Google account. Click on Add, and enter their email address. Click ok, and continue doing this to add more reviewers. When you finish, select the Save button at the top of the page. Your quality reviewers will be able to access your book on their PCs or their reading devices.

Reports / Payment Center / Account Settings

I want to outline the other three selections you see under Google Play in the far-left column of your screen.

Analytics and reports, lets you pull up reports about your book traffic and sales. The most irritating thing about Google is they do not have a sales dashboard. Because of that, it is a hassle to review your sales and earnings. Each time you want to check sales you need to generate a new report and download it as an Excel spreadsheet. Can you say irritating? Hopefully, the folks at Google will figure this one out and make it more user-friendly.

You need to complete the information in payment center before your books can live on Google. To get started, click on the payment center tab. Click on Add Payment profile. Give your payment profile a name, and fill in the information asked for – name, address, etc.

The first thing you need to do is establish your payment settings. By default, you are set up to receive monthly payments with a $1.00 payment threshold. You can change your payment threshold to another dollar amount. You can have Google hold your payments for a specified period (up to one year). After you complete this step, click on Add new bank account. Before you finish setting up your bank account, you need to wait for Google to make a test deposit to your account. When you see the deposit made into your account, click on Add new bank account to verify the deposit amount.

Next, you need to click on billing profile. Click on edit, and scroll down to tax profile. Enter your tax information in the online W9 form.

Scroll down to sales territories. Click on add a territory. Select a payment profile from the drop-down menu. In the choose territories section most often you will type in "world." If you only hold rights in specific areas, click on the question mark. It tells you how to set up individual territories. If you are subject to fixed pricing laws in any of the countries, put a check mark in the box. If not, leave this box blank. Click on enable this region configuration and select create territory.

The final section is Account Settings. Use it to ensure your contact information is correct or to make any changes.

From sign up to verification of my account to listing my books, it took about seven days for my books to show up on Google.

Royalty rates and payments

I could not find any mention of royalties in the Google Play FAQs. When I searched for it in their help section, it said there were no help pages for that topic. I do not know about anybody else, but that scares me.

FYI: I sold my first book on Google Play three days after it went live. I set my list price at $4.99. Google discounted it to $3.60. They paid an after-tax royalty based on a $3.00 selling price, so my royalty worked out to $1.56, or 52 percent. Lesson learned: Add at least $2.00 to your sale price to ensure you receive the payout you expect. The result is I made fifty cents less than I would have received selling the same book for $2.99 on Amazon.

The good news is Google pays thirty days after you make a sale, not sixty days like Amazon and Barnes and Noble. And, they pay at the beginning of the month, not at the end of the month like all other e-publishers.

Self-editing Simplified

I do not know about you. I do not have the time or money to hire an editor.

In the past, that has created some nasty situations. It has gotten me some bad reviews. "The information was interesting, but the author really needs a proofreader. His punctuation is really bad in places." Or, "Very interesting book, but the grammar was driving me crazy. So many commas and semicolons where they do not belong."

Those reviews were a wake-up call.

In 20K A Day, Jonathan Green called them the "kiss of death." His thought is a one-star review that mentions typos and bad grammar is going to kill your book.

Those reviews almost made me give up writing. I mean, I had to think about what I wanted to do. My books have always sold. I am no Stephen King. I never will be. But, a lot of people like my books.

Finally, I sucked it up. I admitted I had a problem. I bought Grammarly, ProWritingAid, and Hemingway. They changed the way I write.

They have my back. These programs keep me from looking like a total hack.

Grammarly and ProWritingAid catch my mistakes. They keep me from looking stupid. Hemingway dumbs my writing down so anyone can understand it.

Together, they make my writing more readable.

Grammarly catches typos, grammatical, and punctuation errors. It makes it look like I know what I am doing. It makes it look like I know my craft and understand the basics of grammar and punctuation. Hemingway strips your writing down to the bare essentials. It took my book from a ninth grade to a fourth-grade level. After a run through Hemingway, anyone can understand my book. There are no big words or complicated sentences for readers to stumble over.

Grammarly is a harsh master.

I use the *Word* plugin. As soon as you enable Grammarly, your screen splits into two boxes. The one to the left is for your document. The box to the right contains Grammarly's suggested edits. Within a few moments, your document is going to light up with red and green underscores. Each underscore has a corresponding edit in the Grammarly box.

Your mission, should you choose to accept it, is to make the red and green go away.

I am going to talk about how to use Grammarly with the Word plugin. If you copy and paste your text into the Grammarly editor, everything works the same.

There is a multitude of errors that can show up in the Grammarly box. I cannot cover them all, but here are some of the key challenges I have had.

I end a lot of sentences with prepositions. Grammarly says some readers may object to that. They suggest that you rewrite the sentence to eliminate problems. Easier said than done. If I am lucky, I can do it one out of three times.

Grammarly says slang is inappropriate and may offend some readers. The same goes for gender snafus. If you write businessman or fireman, it says you should use business person or fire person. Not gonna happen!

Commas are my most significant area for improvement. I put them where they do not belong, and do not put them where they belong. What is worse, Word shows me something different. And, ProWritingAid may contradict Word. If these three programs cannot agree, all I can do is take my best shot. Typically, I read the offending sentence to my seventeen-year-old "Grammar Nazi" and accept her decision.

Grammarly highlights overused words and makes suggestions. Sometimes its suggestions are dead on. Sometimes they miss the mark entirely. It suggested I substitute "read" for "understand." I do not see the connection.

If you misspell a word, it highlights it and shows you the suggested spelling. Do not just click and make the change. Grammarly is not always right. Sometimes it picks the wrong word or a different form of the word. For "understand" it might suggest "understands" or "understanding." It still takes the human touch to get it right.

Sometimes its suggestions are right on. I wrote "Not only does it introduce readers to you, but..." Grammarly suggested, "Not only does it introduce readers to you, but it also..."

Unclear antecedent is one of the more troubling errors. Grammarly does not like it when you start a statement with "they." It wants you to state who "they" are.

Sometimes it suggests you should change words or phrases. It told me to use "more difficult," then a minute later it had me go back to "harder to read." Which one is right? Why the sudden change of mind?

The plagiarism checker catches bits and pieces it can match to websites. When that happens, it suggests how to cite the information.

My biggest problem with the plagiarism checker is it catches single sentences or sentence fragments. Sometimes they are famous sayings that everybody uses. Why would I cite them? Much of this book was first published on my blog.

It nailed it in those instances, so, no doubt, the plagiarism checker works.

Grammarly is not just for books. It can clean up your online image, too.

When you Download the Chrome extension, Grammarly pops up whenever you write online. I use it to edit my blog posts, Facebook posts, and Tweets. I love the smartphone version. It fixes all those stupid autocorrect errors, especially when I am texting or using my Notes app.

Every week, Grammarly emails you a critique of your writing. It tells you how many unique words you wrote that week and how you compare to other writers. It lists your top three errors. Mine are always the same. Misplaced commas, prepositions at the end of the sentence, and unclear antecedent.

What is your biggest writing problem? You will not know until you give Grammarly a whirl.

Final thoughts.

1. Turn Grammarly off when you write. It is irritating to have your document light up in red and green while you're writing. Edit when you finish writing.
2. Edit small bites. I tend to enable Grammarly and go through a 200 or 300-page document all at once. Grammarly cannot handle it. It is slow and clunky if you overload the interface.

3. Word and Grammarly are not a perfect match. When you enable Grammarly, Word gets unstable. Often, I am forced to dump the document I am working on and restart Word. Sometimes it saves my document. Other times, it is back to the drawing board. Lesson learned: Save your work often.
4. Grammarly does not replace a human editor. It cleans up 80 percent of your document. The other 20 percent requires human intervention.

I have a love-hate relationship with Hemingway.

It is slow. It is clunky. The interface is horrible. I could go on. But, it works. It forces me to slash my run-on sentences until the yellow or purple go away. It challenges me to get rid of all the big words and adjectives. It took this book from a ninth-grade to a fourth-grade level. I know, that sounds bad, but the book is so much easier to read.

The dumbing down. Is it good?

I have wrestled with that one, over-and-over. Hemingway fought me with simple words like "require." It highlighted it in purple. It said I should use "need" or "must." It threw a fit when I typed "eliminate." It suggested simpler words like "cut," "drop," and "end." But, it did not flag "antecedent." What the hell?

Two words I overuse are "just" and "really." Hemingway highlights them in blue to let me know they are on the do not use list. Adverbs are bad. They recommend that you use fewer than one for every eighty words.

Ugh!

In case you are wondering. The original text for this chapter started out at the ninth-grade level. After several runs through Hemingway, it is at the third-grade level.

Is that too low?

I am not sure. It is a quick, easy read. Anyone can understand it and put the advice in it into action. That is what writing is all about, right?

Okay. Enough bitching and moaning.

You want to know how Hemingway works and if it is the right tool for you.

Hemingway is a text editor.

You can import documents into it from Word, or you can copy and paste text into it. If you want, it has a "write" mode so that you can use it as your word processor. I would not recommend that. Except for the shortest documents, it would be a pain in the ass.

The right-hand column is the heart of Hemingway. The first box tells you how easy your text is to read. It does that by assigning a grade level. From what I have seen, lower is better. Hemingway likes it when you write at the third to sixth-grade level. More people can understand it.

Below this, it shows your word count. I can start out with one thousand words, By the time I make all my cuts, my document can be 800 words or less. It is hard to make those highlights go away.

What highlights you ask?

Hemingway examines five areas of your writing. It looks for adverbs, the use of passive voices, and words that have more straightforward meanings. It highlights hard to read sentences, and harder to read sentences.

What are adverbs? They are words that modify verbs or adjectives. Most of them end in -ly. By themselves, they are not bad. People tend to overuse them. They tell you things you already know. "Billy is tired." Versus "Billy is really tired." Both sentences mean the same thing. "Really" is an extra word in the second sentence. It does not do anything. So, why not get rid of it?

Hemingway does not tell you that adverbs are bad. It warns you if you use too many of them. When you hover over an adverb, you get the option to click [omit]. Do not do it. There must be a glitch. When I click on omit, it garbles the word instead of deleting it.

Not cool.

Use of passive voice is another biggie that can kill your writing. Whenever possible, use action verbs to move the story forward. "Is," "was," "has been," and "are." We use them all the time.

They are passive. There is not any action. Which sentence sounds better? "Nick is climbing the hill." Or, "Nick climbed the hill."

The last sentence sounds better. It shows Nick in action. A lot of writers get lazy. They do not realize how many times they use passive verbs, so they let them slide by.

Hemingway and Grammarly point out passive voices. Hemingway tells you how many times you use them and how many are okay.

The next one bothers me. Phrases that have simpler meanings.

I understand not everyone owns a dictionary. Not everyone went to college. But, some of the words Hemingway flags do not make sense. Who does not understand "require," "modify," or "examine?"

It is crazy!

But, it is brilliant. When you reread your document after you make the substitutions, it flies by. There is no confusion. You do not stumble over words.

Again, hover your cursor over the highlighted word. A box opens. It displays several words you can substitute. Click on the one you want to use. Better yet, manually make the correction. There is less chance of errors.

You do not have to change every word Hemingway flags, but the more of them you revise, the easier it is to read your book.

It highlights sentences that are hard to read in tan. Check each sentence carefully. Sometimes you can get by with just chopping one or two words. Other times, you need to work at it. Phrases or unnecessary words at the beginning of the sentence can be problematic. I have a habit of beginning sentences with "basically" or "necessarily." When you get rid of these words, many times the highlight disappears. Other phrases we like to stick at the beginning of sentences can cause problems. Some of these are, "I think," "in my opinion," or "in many cases." Get rid of these qualifiers, and the highlight disappears. The funny thing is when you reread the sentence; it sounds better. It is easier to understand.

The final category is very hard to read sentences. Many of these occur when you use quotes. People tend to go on and on when they are talking. Run-on sentences are typical. If it's an interview you conducted, the sentences are easy to correct. When you use a historical quote, things get more complicated.

I tried using Hemingway with a chapter from one of my history books.

What a mess.

Abe Lincoln talked in circles. George Washington's writing is annoying and confusing as hell. The only way to correct it and kill the purple highlights is to pick and choose the portions of the quote you want to use. Sometimes that works. Sometimes it changes the meaning of the quote. Then readers start flagging you for taking liberties with Lincoln.

Sorry, Mr. President.

My best advice is to use Hemingway to clean up what you can if you are editing historical or scientific writing. Use it to clean up your editorial comments. Leave Lincoln and Washington alone.

Your book will still be more readable.

What bothers me the most is Grammarly, Hemingway, and Word do not play well together.

They do not agree on a lot of things. Grammarly makes you remove a comma. Word says you should add it. Word says you should hyphenate a word. Grammarly thinks you should not.

Who is right? Who is wrong?

That is a good question. And, it is one we cannot answer. Many grammar and punctuation rules are not hard and fast. They leave room for personal interpretation.

Do the best you can, then move on. Your document is going to be 99 percent better than when you started. That is a good thing. Celebrate it.

Maybe I Got It All Wrong?

This is the tough part.

What if everything I wrote in this book is a bunch of bullshit and none of it is going to do you any good?

Does it piss you off that I saved this until last?

I know it would get my goat. And, believe me, I am feeling it right now. I discovered a book that could change the way I approach book marketing. Because, maybe, free is not the best solution. And, perhaps ad-stacking 99 cent deals is not going to grow my readership the way I expect.

What would you say if I told you a free-giveaway messes with Amazon's algorithms? Yes, your book takes off at first, but after the initial burst in sales—it sputters out.

What do you do then?

Chris Fox thinks he has the answer. You can read more about it in his <u>Six-Figure Author: Using Data to Sell Books</u>.

What it comes down to is that you do not need a massive launch. You need to get the right people to download your book when you first release it.

Here is the deal.

Amazon algorithms are data-driven. They look for connections between your book and other books in your genre.

A free launch skews the data because your book is not downloaded by its real audience. Instead, it gets picked up by freebie seekers. If you do not believe me, look at Amazon's recommendations after a free run. My books are about history. The books Amazon displays are about gardening, dieting, and cozy mysteries.

Wtf!

None of the people Amazon is recommending my book to are going to buy it. It is not the type of book they read. Any idiot can see that. As a long-term marketing solution, a free promo is a dud. It does not drive sales over the long haul.

And, that comes back to what Jonathan Green says in *20K A Day*, Amazon wants to see a steady increase in sales. They do not want to see a quick burst of downloads, and then a just as quick trickle down.

If you run a promo—KDP Free Days, Countdown Deal, or a 99-cent promotion you need to engineer a slow build up in sales.

If you run a three-day KDP Free promo, do not lead off with your big guns. Start with a smaller promotion on bknights or James H. Mayfield. That should net you 200 to 400 downloads.

Step it up the next day with a promo on Choosy Bookworm. Then come out blasting with your big guns on day three. Shoot for a Robin Reads or FreeBooksy slot.

If you are running a 99-cent promo or Countdown deal, advertise it with bknights on your first day. On day two, blast out an add with Buck Books or BargainBooksy. Save your heavy-hitter for day three. Give it your best shot on Robin Reads or BookBub.

With either promo, announce it to your email list on the last day. This sequence ensures a steady buildup in your sales. It makes Amazon see that your sales are growing.

If you lead off with your strongest promo, Amazon is going to think your ship has already sailed. Instead of a steady stream of sales, Amazon may assume your book fell off the cliff.

The real trick is to get away from free promos as quick as you can. Spend your first year or two building your backlist. Create an email list. Do not try to sign everyone up. One hundred true-fans are better than ten thousand lukewarm names. What you want to shoot for is a list of readers you can count on to download your book the first day you release it. This is going to do two things for you. It is going to raise your sales rank and visibility. That is money in your pocket.

Money is good.

Those first few purchases are going to prime the pump. They are going to teach Amazon who your real readers are. Once Amazon discovers this information, its marketing engine kicks in. Amazon is going to promote your book to its true audience, not some mixed bag of free book seekers.

This is a lot to take in.

It is the exact opposite of what everyone says you should do. But, it makes sense. Amazon's sales engine is data-driven. If you have bought enough stuff from them, they are excellent at suggesting what comes next.

I get email suggestions every day. I do not buy every one of them, but I do purchase my fair share.

Final Wrap-up

In the immortal words of the Looney Tunes, "That's all folks!"

Thank you for hanging in there until the end. I know it has been a long ride.

If I could give you just one piece of advice, it would be to hang in there and keep writing.

Sometimes an author gets lucky. Their first book takes off and starts selling like hotcakes from the get-go. But, most times it is a slow process. You publish a book on Kindle or Smashwords. When you check your sales dashboard – Nothing shows up. Nothing at all.

A week goes by, and you sell one or two books. Another week, and two, or three more sales trail in. Maybe mom finally bought a copy, or perhaps an old-school mate in Davenport or Clinton (hint!) heard about your book and decided to give it a read.

The fact is building an audience takes time. Building an audience that likes your books takes even longer.

The best advice I can give you is to write your book. Spend a few days promoting it. Start writing another book. Repeat the process. Over time you will sell more books.

When I was a full-time eBay seller I had good weeks and bad weeks. I could not do anything to make the bad weeks better. All I knew was if I continued to do the right stuff more sales would follow. Writing and self-publishing is a lot like that.

Keep writing. Make your books available in as many formats as possible. eBooks, paperbacks, and audiobooks are easy enough to produce.

If you write nonfiction, keep updating your older books. Ensure that they stay current. Publish new editions every year or so.

You never know what is going to happen.

I have books that never sold over ten copies on Kindle. Out of the blue someone orders fifty or a hundred copies in paperback. As soon as I added audiobooks to the puzzle, they began to sell hundreds of copies per month.

It is crazy but true. If you publish enough books – You could become an overnight sensation.

Keep writing.

Read These Books Next

My original idea was to write a book titled *57 Must-Read Books for Self-Publishers*. Over time it morphed into my blog, *indie author's toolbox*, and then this book.

I have read almost every book written about self-publishing. Many of them have been helpful; a few have raised more questions than they answered. I finally narrowed my recommended reading list down to these ten books.

I only chose one book by Steve Scott. But, any of his books would be a good starting point for new authors.

If you are new to the writing game, any of Rob Parnell's *The Easy Way to Write* guides would be enlightening. Rob is a great guy who is passionate about helping writers improve their skills. While you are at it, check out his wife's book. It's called, <u>Show Don't Tell, The Ultimate Writer's Guide</u>. Her name is Robyn Opie Parnell, and her book is an excellent primer on how to bring your writing to life.

Martin Crosbie is a novelist and the author of <u>How I Sold 30,000 eBooks on Amazon's Kindle</u>. Martin is on a mission to help other writers. It shines through in his blog, his books, and every action he takes.

My thanks go out to Norm Schriever. He was the first of many interviews for my blog. I caught up with Norm while he was traveling through Southeast Asia. His book, <u>The Book Marketing Bible</u> has a lot of great tips and tricks for self-publishers.

Finally, I want to thank the dynamic duo of Buck Flogging – Matt Stone and Rob Archangel. Their book, <u>Kill Your Blog</u> got me started contacting other authors. Here is the magical advice, direct from their book, "email somebody. Send them a direct message on Facebook. Call those fools."

Now I ask you, what could be more inspiring than that? Who would have figured all I had to do was shoot someone an email, and they would drop everything to help me out?

This is for all the authors who take time out to help the newbies along the way.

As Mr. Spock would say, "May you live long, and prosper."

<u>Writing Habit Mastery</u>. S. J. Scott (alias Steve Scott). Time management and motivation are the two most significant stumbling blocks for authors. This book gives a lot of great practical advice to get you writing and keep you cranking out book after book.

What amazes me about Steve is he is so open in all his books and blog posts. The one thing he always talks about is giving readers value for the money they invest in his books. Other writers speak of price pulsing, so they can make the most money from their books. Steve is always out there pitching his books at 99¢, $2.99, or free. And, when you hear him talk about his numbers this strategy has paid off better over the long haul.

<u>Six-Figure Author: Using Data to Sell Books</u>. Chris Fox. I mentioned this book in the previous chapter. It is one of those books that is going to give you an ah-ha moment. Sean Platt and Johnnie B. Truant talk about how you only need 1,000 true-fans. David Gaughran unravels Amazon algorithms so that you can hit Amazon's lists and sell more books.

Chris Fox fills in the blanks. He explains Amazon Algorithms in more detail. He teaches you how to train Amazon so that it hooks your book up with interested readers.

Read all three books so that you understand how the pieces fit together. The key thing that comes out is that an email list is essential to your author success. And, the biggest list is not always the best. It is more important to have readers who connect with you. Your style. And, your unique outlook.

The same goes for sales.

Not all sales are equal. Most authors shoot for the most sales possible. Fox says they are going about it all wrong. When you launch your book, it is not the number of sales you make. It is the number of buyers who match your unique customer avatar.

Say it with me. I am doing it all wrong, and I am going to change. Or, at least, rethink what I am doing.

Write. Publish. Repeat. Sean Platt and Johnnie B. Truant. Hands down this is the best book about self-publishing. These guys hit on every topic from content creation to publishing and marketing. Key takeaways are to concentrate on finding your real fans. They will do the marketing for you.

And, like the title says: write, publish, and repeat. Putting more content out there is one sure way to help you get discovered and sell more books.

Let's Get Visible. David Gaughran. This book offers excellent advice on how to get your book noticed. It talks about how to battle the "sales cliff." That is the point where your book stalls out. Where it seems like getting sales is harder than pulling teeth. It explains Amazon algorithms so that you understand how to get the power of Amazon behind your book. Another section details pricing and price pulsing.

How I Sold 30,000 eBooks on Amazon's Kindle, An Easy-to-Follow Self-Publishing Guide. Martin Crosbie. "Everything leads to something else, and you never know who might be reading your work or watching your career."

For Martin, writing books resulted in speaking, teaching, and writing more books. Who knows where your writing will take you? His other advice is you are going to need more than one book—so keep writing.

I revisited this one again last night. Every author needs to spend some time with it. Martin's attitude is remarkable. He does everything he can to help newer writers learn the trade. Each step along the way he tried new things and reached out to help others. Each time he did this, new doors opened for him – writing, teaching, or some other method to help promote his books.

Like it. Hate it. It doesn't matter. Read it. Start giving back to move your career forward.

How to Sell Video Courses online, How I Earn $1000+ a Month While I Sleep. Rob Cubbon. Rob's book is not about writing or self-publishing. But, for some writers, it could lead to one of those ah-ha moments. It could help them move beyond books to email or online courses. The book is easy to read and a good starting point if you were thinking about online instruction.

I interviewed Rob for my blog a while back. Here is one of the tips he shared. "Turning an eBook into a course is one of the easiest things because you already have the content and structure. Here's what you do. Condense every chapter of your Kindle into a few slides in PowerPoint. Use ScreenFlow or Camtasia to film the slides while you use your book to narrate over them. It's easy to 'ad lib' whilst you're reading your text."

Learn Amazon Ads: Use AMS to Find More Readers and Sell More Books. Mark J. Dawson and Joseph Alexander. Mark Dawson is the go-to guy for Amazon and Facebook ads.

Everybody is experimenting with Amazon ads. No one is sure how they work. (Except maybe, Mark.) Some authors have an eighteen percent ACOS (Amazon Cost of Sales). Others are closer to one-hundred percent. The difference is how they target and track their ads.

Mark breaks down Amazon ads. He explains how to target your audience with deadly precision. He shares tips and tricks to make your campaigns more successful. His top tip is to run more ads. It is a no-brainer. Spending money on Amazon ads is hard. You can set your spending target at $100 per day, yet Amazon barely takes $2.00.

What gives? Most books have a small target audience. To get Amazon to reach more people you need to run more ads and target different keywords.

20K a Day: How to Launch More Books and Make More Money By Writing Faster, Better, and Smarter. Jonathan Green. I cannot believe I am recommending this book. There are so many things I dislike about it. It is repetitive. It rambles. The author goes on, and on, about his beach house. It is irritating. But, I learned a few tricks from it.

I bought Hemingway and dumbed my books down. It took this one from a ninth-grade level down to fourth-grade. By helping me get rid of the big words, compound sentences, and run-on sentences—it made it so much more readable.

It also made me want to try dictating my books using Dragon Dictation. It is a free app for iPhone, and it is so damn cool. Unlike software that converts PDF documents to Word, this shit works. From the get-go, it is over ninety percent accurate. I click the button to start recording. When I finish, it takes a few seconds to do its magic. Then I email it to myself, and I have a blog post or chapter with minimal rewriting.

I love this shit!

Jonathan Green you are awesome! These ideas are so good that I am going to recommend his other book. Breaking Orbit: How to Write, Publish, and Launch Your First Bestseller on Amazon Without a Mailing List, Blog or Social Media Following.

Write What Sells: Book Writing Guide to Target Niches That Sell for the Indie Author. Alex Foster. This book provides down to Earth practical advice to help you sell more books. It is all summed up in this one sentence. "General books don't sell, specific books do."

Enough said. It is a short, easy read. It will help you choose topics that sell. Read it. Put what you learn into practice. Sell more books.

Guerilla Publishing: Revolutionary Book Marketing Strategies. Derek Murphy. This one got off to a bumpy start. Murphy released the first version with his rough draft. Once he got that corrected, things picked up.

This is a book about breaking the rules.

Murphy says, "The easiest way to fail is to do everything you hear."

Like Jonathan Green, Murphy tells readers you do not need to be the best writer. You just need to write "what readers want to read."

And, how do you find out what people want to read about? You read books in your genre so that you understand what makes them tick.

It is true. You have got to read, to write.

I read three to five books a week outside of the topics I am researching and writing about. They expose me to different approaches and writing styles. They make me think. Each book is an ah-ha moment. I never knew that. I did not know I could do that.

If you want to write better books, read more books.

There are a lot of other books out there about writing, self-publishing and how to build a raving fan base. I owe a debt to them all. I would like to apologize for not having time or space to mention them.

Know this: I appreciate your time and effort.

Thank-you very much!

About the Author

My books offer short easy to read solutions to your e-commerce problems.

You can read most of them in under an hour. The information will help you sell more products on eBay and Amazon. It will help you sell more services on Fiverr, or eBooks on Amazon and Kindle.

Selling online is not a mystery. It does not have to be difficult. It is all about getting started. Many people I have talked with have this crazy fear of putting things up for sale on eBay and Amazon. Somehow, they get the idea they need to do this or that. They worry they do not know enough about what they are doing to do it right. They wonder what they should sell, and about whether they can even do it or not.

That is where my books come in. They take you hand in hand and walk you through getting started selling on eBay,

Amazon, Etsy, and Fiverr. They show you how to market your Kindle books.

My goal is to get you over the speed bumps so that you can be more successful from the get-go. What are you waiting for?

Most of my books are available as audiobooks.

July 1st, 2017

Nick Vulich

Davenport, Iowa

If you enjoyed this book

Thank you for reading this book. If you liked it or found it helpful, I would be grateful if you would post a review. Your review does help. It helps other readers decide if this book would help them on their writing journey. It helps me to make this an even better book for you. I read all the reviews my books receive. Based on what readers tell me, I can make my books even better. I do my best to include the kind of information readers want and need.

Thanks again for choosing my book. Here's wishing you success.

https://www.amazon.com/dp/B072J2661G/ref=sr_1_1?s=digital-text&ie=UTF8&qid=1494983466&sr=1-1&keywords=writable

Want to know about Nick's new book releases? Join our mailing list.

Interested in knowing when Nick releases his next book? Click here to join our mailing list. We promise not to send any spam or unwanted emails. The only thing you will receive is news about Nick's new book releases and occasional specials.

www.ingramcontent.com/pod-product-compliance
Lightning Source LLC
Chambersburg PA
CBHW050443290526
45786CB00006B/2144